"The world was peopled
with wonders."

The origin of Wildsam comes from above, a line of prose in the novel, *East of Eden,* written by John Steinbeck. Six words hinting at a broad and interwoven idea. One of curiosity, connection, joy. And the belief that stories have the power to unearth the mysteries of a place—for anyone. The book in your hands is rooted in such things.

Our sincere thanks to the many people in Charleston who helped our team create this second edition. We're grateful for generosity and insight from Emily Storrow, CJ Lotz, Paul Saylors, Shannon Ravenel, Alicia Boyd, Wesley Verhoeve, Matthew Lambert, Josephine Humphreys, Maggie Brett Kennedy, Brooks Reitz, Jennifer Cole, Olivia Rae James, Will Copenhaver, Will Mischner, Rob and Ginger Carmichael, and Molly Waring. SDCO Partners is the best in the biz, and we are so lucky that their work infuses these pages. Finally, to our first edition city editor, Jessica Mischner, our genuine appreciation for your curiosity and love of all things Charleston.

WILDSAM FIELD GUIDES™

Published in the United States
by Wildsam Field Guides, Austin, Texas.

ISBN 978-1-4671-9952-0

Illustrations by SDCO Partners

To find more field guides, please visit
www.wildsam.com

CONTENTS

Discover the people and places that tell the story of Charleston

WELCOME

THERE ARE DOZENS of great American cities, but only a rare few have a mysterious quality akin to magic. These cities have a feeling, a palpability, a sense of themselves that is immediately personal and manifest. The remembered light of such places still warms the traveler long after leaving.

Charleston is one of the magical few. Walk for ten minutes down Broad Street, then venture south into the rainbow of historic houses, smelling the jasmined walls, hearing the clip-clop of surreys, eyeing the little white boats skimming the harbor. What the Romans called *genius loci* is intense. And inside Charleston's romp of restaurants, from cracker-crumble oyster shacks to smart chefs' quarters, more of the conjuring unfolds. Bowens Island, Bertha's Kitchen, Leon's, Chez Nous, Hannibal's Kitchen, FIG, The Ordinary—these and more institutions, old and new, do more than feed the body. Together with a league of talented growers and watermen, they pass along the very essence of the place.

Just as vital to Charleston's beating heart is the Lowcountry, the *out there*, where the landscape casts an even headier spell. Semi-tropical thickets whirring, saltwater channels running, long gray oaks loping like dinosaurs. As you tunnel deeper into the sea-island world, it's easy to lose your sense of time. The splendor is almost severe.

Charleston is a place with tangled roots and complex flavors. So much of what's essential about the city traces back to its darker lineage. Agriculture, cooking, the building arts, even the warm, lifted accents: each carries reminders of slavery's scarred history—a history that new generations continue to challenge and illuminate. This ongoing reckoning has only grown more urgent and acute in the wake of the 2015 shooting at Mother Emanuel AME.

Charleston's story is the American story in that way. It captures the highest highs and lowest lows, hopes realized and hopes deferred. A Holy City, a flawed city. A city that has captivated for four centuries and that is still learning how to fully tell its own story. And though it may be hard for those of us "from off" to ever fully unlock the spell, that doesn't make the lure any less strong. —The Editors

ESSENTIALS

TRANSPORT

BIKE RENTAL
The Bicycle Shoppe
thebicycleshoppe.com

FREE SHUTTLE
Downtown Area Shuttle
ridecarta.com

PEDICAB
Charleston Pedicab
pedicabcharleston.com

LANDMARKS

ANGEL OAK
3688 *Angel Oak Rd*
Gorgeous old tree's epic branches create sprawling shade.

THE BATTERY
East Battery and Murray Blvd
Seawall and promenade run down to White Point Garden.

MEDIA

NEWSPAPER
The Post and Courier
Oldest daily in the South.

PODCAST
Charleston Time Machine
Historian Nic Butler's deep dives.

MAGAZINE
Garden & Gun
Progressive Southern lifestyle coverage; top-notch writing.

GREENSPACE

JAMES ISLAND COUNTY PARK
871 *Riverland Dr*
Tidal creeks for fishing and crabbing, walking paths and bike trails cover 643 acres.

CALENDAR

- JAN Lowcountry Oyster Festival
- FEB Southeastern Wildlife Exposition
- MAR Charleston Wine + Food
- APR High Water Festival
- MAY North Charleston Arts Fest
- JUN Spoleto Festival
- JUL Sweetgrass Festival
- AUG RiverDogs baseball games
- SEP Lowcountry Jazz Festival
- OCT Fall Tour of Homes
- NOV Steeplechase of Charleston
- DEC *Garden & Gun* Jubilee

FOODWAY

HOPPIN' JOHN
Pork-laced mix of Carolina Gold rice and Sea Island red peas blends Lowcountry agriculture with West African roots.

BOOKS

- *Edisto* by Padgett Powell
- *Charleston Receipts* by The Junior League of Charleston
- *Africanisms of the Gullah Dialect* by Lorenzo Dow Turner

ITINERARY

FRIDAY

Gullah tour with Alphonso Brown
Dinner at Chez Nous
Dancing at The Commodore

SATURDAY

Marina Variety Store breakfast
South of Broad stroll
Art browsing at the Halsey Institute
FIG dinner

SUNDAY

Sullivan's Island morning walk
Leon's lunch
High Wire Distilling tour and tasting

MEMENTOS

No. 12 Southern Magnolia candle, *Charleston Candle Co.*, $22
Sweetgrass basket, *Charleston City Market*, $250
Goldbug pin, *Croghan's Jewel Box*, $70

RECORD COLLECTION

Shovels & Rope .... *Swimmin' Time*
Hootie & the Blowfish .... *Cracked Rear View*
Chubby Checker .... *Cameo Parkway*
The Gullah Kinfolk .... *Songs uv dee Gullah Pee'puls*
Maurice Williams and the Zodiacs .... *Stay*
Band of Horses .... *Cease to Begin*
Mac Arnold & Plate Full O' Blues .... *Country Man*
Iron & Wine .... *Around the Well*
The Marshall Tucker Band .... *The Marshall Tucker Band*
NEEDTOBREATHE .... *Rivers in the Wasteland*
Susto .... *Susto*
Brave Baby .... *Electric Friends*
Ranky Tanky .... *Ranky Tanky*
Corey Smith .... *Carolina*

ESSENTIALS

LODGING

The Dewberry
334 Meeting St
A '50s federal building, midcentury vibe intact. Best rooftop bar view [and drinks] around.

The Restoration
75 Wentworth St
Roomy suites, right off King Street. Browse local wares at on-site shop, The Port.

Zero George
0 George St
Restored colonial homes turned boutique hotel. Sip wine in the shade of one of three historic piazzas.

The Vendue
19 Vendue Range
Charleston's "art hotel" lives up to the name: 300+ pieces throughout the property.

The Spectator
67 State St
Art deco beauty with a classy bar. Personal butler service goes the extra mile.

Emeline
181 Church St
Velvet couches, Matouk linens, locally made Urban Electric lighting. An erstwhile DoubleTree, but you'd never know it.

The Ryder
237 Meeting St
Afternoon plan: a dip in the second-floor pool, oysters and tequila cocktails from Little Palm on the patio.

Hotel Bella Grace
117 Calhoun St
Preservation meets modern touches in a restored mansion across the street from Mother Emanuel AME Church.

Guesthouse Charleston
guesthousecharleston.com
Rebecca Ramsay designs short-term rentals with spacious but cozy living spaces, conveniently clustered for groups.

COFFEE

Second State
Mount Pleasant

The Daily
Cannonborough-Elliottborough

Vintage Coffee Cafe
Mount Pleasant

The Harbinger
North Central

Sightsee Shop + Coffee
Cannonborough-Elliottborough

BOOKSTORES

Blue Bicycle Books
Radcliffeborough

Buxton Books
Harleston Village

Itinerant Literate Bookstop
Park Circle

Preservation Society of Charleston
Harleston Village

ISSUES

Housing	The city is facing a housing crisis, with more than 40 percent of residents funneling at least a third of their income into their homes. A 2021 study estimates that more than 16,000 affordable housing units need to be built by 2030. **EXPERT:** *Geona Shaw Johnson, director, Charleston Department of Housing and Community Development*
Historic Preservation	The cultural sites of Charleston resonate with centuries of dark and complicated stories, many of which have long been suppressed. In recent years, there has been a gradual reckoning, and with it, a shift toward a more honest telling of the former slave trade hub's Black history. **EXPERT:** *Winslow Hastie, president and CEO, Historic Charleston Foundation*
Flooding	The Lowcountry is called that for a reason, and this city built upon a marshy landscape is prone to flooding. High tides and storm surges also erode beaches, leaving homes more vulnerable. Sea-level rise is exacerbating these effects; in the last century, the Atlantic along the coast has risen over a foot. **EXPERT:** *Paul T. Gayes, director, Coastal Carolina University's Burroughs & Chapin Center for Marine and Wetland Studies*
Carriage Tours	As appealingly quaint as the sight of horses clopping down city streets may be, it's also controversial. Animal rights groups are pushing for new regulations. **EXPERT:** *Ellen Harley, co-founder, Charleston Carriage Horse Advocates*

STATISTICS

40% .... Enslaved Africans who passed through Charleston Harbor
43 .... National Historic Landmarks in Charleston County
10 .... Seaside golf holes at Kiawah's Ocean Course, most in hemisphere
7.43 million .... Tourists who visited Charleston in 2019
2.5 .... Length in miles of Arthur Ravenel Jr. Bridge
60% .... Approx. decrease in Charleston's Black population since 1980s
$88 million .... Granted to Mother Emanuel victims' families in 2021

NEIGHBORHOODS

SOUTH OF BROAD

Antebellum ostentation is on full display at the peninsula's southernmost point.

LOCAL: *Burbage's, White Point Garden, Rainbow Row*

FRENCH QUARTER

Named for French Huguenots. Timeless magic is best felt at night in the low flicker of gas lanterns.

LOCAL: *Dock Street Theatre, Blind Tiger Pub, Goat. Sheep. Cow.*

HARLESTON VILLAGE

A respite from tourist-filled King Street, especially along Colonial Lake's walking paths.

LOCAL: *The Cistern Yard, Queen Street Grocery*

EAST SIDE

Historically Black neighborhood with eclectic mix of architecture.

LOCAL: *Hannibal's Kitchen, The Commodore, The Cigar Factory*

CANNONBOROUGH-ELLIOTTBOROUGH

Onetime commerce hub for Jewish families and Black Charlestonians; still diverse and lively.

LOCAL: *Dave's Carry-Out, Sugar Bakeshop, Xiao Bao Biscuit*

WEST ASHLEY

Bustling suburb of post-war bungalows and big-box retail.

LOCAL: *The Glass Onion, Red Orchids China Bistro, GDC Home*

OLD VILLAGE

In the oldest part of Mount Pleasant, hushed, shaded streets lead to dockside seafood shops.

LOCAL: *Post House Inn, Tarvin Seafood, Pitt Street Bridge*

WAGENER TERRACE

Residential enclave anchored by 60-acre Hampton Park, where community spirit runs deep.

LOCAL: *Lowndes Grove, Herd Provisions, Sushi-Wa*

NORTH CENTRAL

Cottages and bungalows sit sidecar to hip restaurants in converted pharmacies and service stations.

LOCAL: *Rodney Scott's BBQ, Redux Contemporary Art Center*

NORTH CHARLESTON

Former naval base is a beacon for new residents and businesses, especially in happening Park Circle.

LOCAL: *Stems & Skins, Jackrabbit Filly, The Bend*

CHARLESTON

NORTH CHARLESTON
WAGENER TERRACE
ASHLEY RIVER
26
NORTH CENTRAL
17
HAMPTON PARK
UPPER KING
THE CITADEL
EAST SIDE
COOPER RIVER
CANNONBOROUGH-ELLIOTTBOROUGH
MARION SQUARE
RADCLIFFEBOROUGH
ANSONBOROUGH
HARLESTON VILLAGE
CITY MARINA
FRENCH QUARTER
SOUTH OF BROAD
THE BATTERY
MCCLELLANVILLE
AWENDAW
26
95
526
DANIEL ISLAND
MOUNT PLEASANT
ISLE OF PALMS
DOWNTOWN
SULLIVAN'S ISLAND
JAMES ISLAND
JOHNS ISLAND
WADMALAW ISLAND
FOLLY BEACH
KIAWAH ISLAND
SEABROOK ISLAND
EDISTO ISLAND
BEAUFORT
SAINT HELENA ISLAND
HUNTING ISLAND

SELECTED CONTENT

BESTS

A curated list of city favorites—classic and new—from bars and restaurants to shops and experiences, plus a handful of can't-miss experts

FOOD & DRINK

For a map of favorite Charleston dishes, see page 56.

OYSTERS

Bowens Island Restaurant
1870 Bowens Island Rd, Bowens Island
Roasted oyster clusters in a generations-old shack over the salt marsh.

FRENCH

Chez Nous
6 Payne Ct
Cannonborough
Restored Charleston single house serving European flavor via the Lowcountry larder.

BARBECUE

Rodney Scott's BBQ
1011 King St
North Central
Local favorite long before Beard awards and Netflix. Eat the pulled pork with white bread like a taco.

NEW AMERICAN

FIG
232 Meeting St
Ansonborough
Meeting Street stalwart. There's a reason the ricotta gnocchi doesn't leave the menu.

MEAT AND THREE

Bertha's Kitchen
2332 Meeting Street Rd, North Charleston
Three sisters serve up fried chicken, collard greens, red beans and rice, cornbread—the works.

GRITS

Millers All Day
120 King St
Lower King
Serves and sells ground goodness from local miller Greg Johnsman—even of the "unicorn" variety.

FRESH CATCH

The Ordinary
544 King St
Cannonborough
Mike Lata's maritime masterwork: tiered seafood towers, gussied up bycatch, rum galore.

ASIAN

Xiao Bao Biscuit
224 Rutledge Ave
Cannonborough
Former gas station where okonomiyaki might as well be Japanese for "Now this is a pancake."

SIMPLE BREAKFAST

Marina Variety Store
17 Lockwood Dr
Harleston Village
Eggs, hashbrowns, bacon, double-buttermilk biscuits by Ashley River docks.

SMALL PLATES

Chubby Fish

252 Coming St

Cannonborough

The fish curry is worth the wait.

ITALIAN

Le Farfalle

15 Beaufain St

Harleston Village

Bustling beaut slings octopus carpaccio and house-made focaccia.

FRIED CHICKEN

Leon's

698 King St

Westside

Old Bay-inflected fried chicken and frozen G&Ts.

VEGGIES

The Grocery

4 Cannon St

Cannonborough

Kevin Johnson's paean to all things local, turnips to triggerfish.

BAR MENU

Little Jack's Tavern

710 King St

Westside

Clever throwback complete with shrimp cocktail and a lauded burger.

FRIED SEAFOOD

Dave's Carry-Out

42 Morris St

Cannonborough

No-frills spot earns its cult following. Always add a deviled crab.

BAKERY

EVO Craft Bakery

1075 E Montague Ave

North Charleston

Top-notch crusty loaf. Wood-fired pizzeria up front is tops too.

FISH SANDWICH

CudaCo.

765 Folly Rd

James Island

The creekside fish shop sandwich of your dreams.

SOUTHERN SEAFOOD

Hannibal's Kitchen

16 Blake St

East Side

One word: ethereal. A 40-plus-year neighborhood institution.

APERITIF

Babas on Cannon

11 Cannon St

Cannonborough

Grab a sidewalk table for house-bottled negronis and salty snacks.

DIVE BAR

The Griffon

18 Vendue Range

French Quarter

Sip cheap drinks, shoot darts. Dollar bills paper the walls.

COURTYARD

Blind Tiger Pub

36-38 Broad St

French Quarter

Broad Street icon named for a speakeasy synonym.

COCKTAILS

Doar Bros.

225 Meeting St

Ansonborough

Cocktails like the Burn District nod to local stories of yore.

WINE LIST

Bin 152

152 King St

Lower King

Thirty by the glass, 100 by the bottle, all on a peaceful stretch of lower King.

BEER LIST

Edmund's Oast

1081 Morrison Dr

Wagener Terrace

Euro-inspired beer hall with 20 house-brewed taps.

SHOPPING

MEN'S STYLE

Indigo & Cotton
79 Cannon St
Cannonborough
Smart selection of small-batch brands like Raleigh Denim, Gitman Bros. and Billykirk.

DESIGN

Fritz Porter Design Collective
701 E Bay St
East Side
Emporium of antiques, designer wares and fine linens in the Cigar Factory.

SURF

McKevlin's Surf
8 Center St
Folly Beach
Refuge for the sea-sprayed, with rentals, lessons and Folly surf reports. Among the country's oldest.

BAIT AND TACKLE

Blue Water Tackle Shop
1880 F Andell Bluff Blvd, Johns Island
Cold beer, fishing licenses, crickets and minnows to last all weekend.

JEWELRY

Croghan's Jewel Box
308 King St
King St Historic Dist.
The 100-year-old family business trades in estate jewels and silver rice spoons.

WOMEN'S BOUTIQUE

Hampden Clothing
314 King St
King St Historic Dist.
Style with runway flair curated by the city's queen of chic. Nearly 10,000 sq ft after 2020 expansion.

OUTFITTER

Half-Moon Outfitters
280 King St
King St Historic Dist.
Where paddlers and campers and other outdoors-folks get Lowcountry intel.

CANDLES

Candlefish
270 King St
King St Historic Dist.
Hand-poured soy candles in an apothecary-style shop opened by Rewined founders.

CHEESE

Goat. Sheep. Cow.
106 Church St
South of Broad
Modern cheese-monger in a 200-year-old building. Clutch for impromptu picnicking.

PAPER GOODS

Social Paper Co

826 Coleman Blvd

Mt Pleasant

Stationery, letterpress cards, gifts. Custom work, too.

SEAFOOD

Abundant Seafood

248 Magwood Ln

Mount Pleasant

Dockside counter by the fisherman supplying the city's top chefs.

BUTCHER

Ted's Butcherblock

334 E Bay St

Ansonborough

Meats and seafood with pedigree. A cafe menu too.

CLASSIC STYLE

Berlin's Clothing

114 King St

Harleston Village

Fixture since 1883, when owner Henry Berlinski arrived with $1.38 in his pocket.

ART SUPPLIES

Artist & Craftsman

981 King St

North Central

Three floors in a former church fuel the city's creatives.

WINE

Graft Wine Shop

700 King St

Westside

Femi Oyediran and Miles White's temple of natty wine and fresh beats.

SMALL GROCER

Veggie Bin

96 Spring St

Cannonborough-Ell.

From tortillas to kombucha to Clemson blue cheese.

SWEETS

Sugar Bakeshop

59 1/2 Cannon St

Cannonborough

Small-batch goodness. Seasonal cupcakes are winners.

PRODUCE

Legare Farms

2620 Hanscombe Pt Rd, Johns Island

Long history [1725] on 300 acres along the Stono River.

FURNITURE

Celadon Home

1015 Johnnie Dodds Blvd, Mount Pleasant

Furnishings and decor for the modern world traveler.

ANTIQUES

Wynsum Antiques & Interiors

648 King St

Westside

Treasures don't have to break the bank.

BEAUTY

Old Whaling Company

409 King St

Radcliffeborough

Fragrant, sea-inspired soap and bath bombs.

CHILDREN'S SHOP

Under the Almond Trees

190 King St

Lower King

Pint-size fashion, baby goods galore.

BICYCLES

The Bicycle Shoppe

280 Meeting St

King St Historic Dist.

Gear and guidance for pedaling the peninsula, since 1986.

MODERN GIFT

Fieldshop

344 Meeting St

Wraggborough

Garden & Gun editors curate this sunny corner of The Dewberry Hotel.

ACTION

For maps of art institutions and beaches, see pages 66 and 68.

BASEBALL
RiverDogs
360 Fishburne St
Westside
Farm club for the Tampa Bay Rays. Keep an eye out for adopted local Bill Murray in the stands.

WALKING TOUR
Walk & Talk Charleston
walkandtalkchs.com
Meet at Church Street's *Hat Man* mural for a stroll centered on the city and its characters.

SECRET BEACH
Capers Island
dnr.sc.gov
Where ospreys and loggerheads nest among driftwood remains. Accessible only by boat.

FISHING
Drum Runner Charters
56 Ashley Point Dr
West Ashley
Inshore flats or fly fishing in estuaries and tidal creeks; learn how to cast a shrimp net.

SAILING
Charleston Sailing Adventures
10 Wharfside St
Ansonborough
See the city from 27-foot catamaran *Prevailing Winds*. Look out for dolphins.

CINEMA
Terrace Theater
1956 Maybank Hwy
James Island
Snack on caramel cake and wine while watching foreign and indie flicks.

PLAYHOUSE
Footlight Players
20 Queen St
French Quarter
Launched in 1931 with one-act plays; now Lowcountry's community theater in a converted cotton warehouse.

SPIRITS
High Wire Distilling
311 Huger St
North Central
Tour from mash to still; sample sorghum whiskey, watermelon brandy, barrel-rested gin.

CRABBING
Casual Crabbing with Tia
casualcrabbingwithtia.com
Hit the docks with a local who grew up with crabbing in her blood.

FARM STAND

Rosebank Farms
4362 Betsy Kerrison Pkwy, Johns Island
Mom-and-pop-style stand. Farming since the 18th century.

LIVE MUSIC

Charleston Music Hall
37 John St Wraggborough
Listening room disguised as a Gothic Revival concert hall.

FINE ART

Gallery Row
Broad St French Quarter
First Friday art walks every month.

DANCING

The Commodore
504 Meeting St East Side
Rollicking reincarnation of '80s jazz club A Touch of Class.

LATE NIGHT

The Faculty Lounge
391 Huger St Westside
Private club with lounge-style bar and courtyard. One-night membership, $10.

NATURE PRESERVE

Center for Birds of Prey
4719 Hwy 17 N Awendaw
Tour an avian rehab facility and watch raptor flight demos.

MORNING JOG

Hampton Park
30 Mary Murray Dr Wagener Terrace
Green space full of antique roses and oak-lined footpaths.

MUSEUM

Gibbes Museum of Art
135 Meeting St French Quarter
Southern masterpieces old and new.

PUBLIC GARDEN

White Point Garden
2 Murray Blvd South of Broad
Civil War remnants, big harbor views.

DRIVE

Charleston to Rockville
Maybank Hwy
Cross Wadmalaw Island under moss-draped live oaks to salt-marsh banks.

CARRIAGE TOURS

Palmetto Carriage
8 Guignard St French Quarter
Entertaining, accurate tours. Touristy but worth it.

COOKING CLASSES

In the Kitchen with Chef Bob Waggoner
164 Market St Lower King
Dinner party-style classes with a gregarious host.

GYM

The Works
465 Meeting St East Side
The city's infamous heat has nothing on yoga-cardio classes at this "sweat studio."

SUP

Charleston Outdoor Adventures
1871 Bowens Island Rd, Bowens Island
Explore tidal creeks and learn about the resident critters.

SUNDAY HANG

Station 19
Sullivan's Island
Flat beach for frisbee tosses, sunny naps.

EXPERTISE

LANDSCAPE ARCHITECT

Glen Gardner

gardnerla.com

Charleston native with deep roots and a focus on the botany of the Palmetto State. Lush gardens, small to sprawling.

CONSERVATION

Andrew Wunderley

@chaswaterkeeper

Longtime protective voice of Lowcountry aqua-ecosystems, from salt marsh to tidal creeks and oyster beds.

FARM SUSTAINABILITY

GrowFood Carolina

growfoodcarolina.com

A produce hub that aggregates, markets and sells produce for area growers. The goal: to protect small family farms.

LIGHTING DESIGN

Urban Electric Company

urbanelectricco.com

Dedicated to illuminating Charleston—and the rest of the world—with style and craftsmanship.

SWEETGRASS WEAVING

Corey Alston

Charleston City Market Ansonborough

Lacing together sweetgrass, bulrush, pine needles and palmetto leaves. A Gullah tradition.

GULLAH GEECHEE

Victoria Smalls

@WeBeGullah

Cultural preservationist heads up nonprofit Gullah Geechee Cultural Heritage Corridor Commission.

PRESERVATION

Glenn Keyes

glennkeyesarchitects.com

National leader in preservation of historic structures. Citywide portfolio includes City Market, Aiken-Rhett House.

CULINARY HISTORIAN

Kevin Mitchell

@[illegible]

Champions the undersung legacies of free and enslaved Black cooks, including 19th-century cook Nat Fuller.

POET LAUREATE

Marcus Amaker

@charlestonpoet

Charleston's first poet laureate is also a musician and the lead graphic designer for music magazine *No Depression*.

MARINE SUPPLY

Charleston's Rigging

charlestonsrigging.com

Everything you need to get—and keep—your boat afloat.

TATTOO

Blu Gorilla

blugorilla.com

Chucktown's first tat shop has still got it.

FLORIST

Roadside Blooms

roadsideblooms.com

Designs emphasize foraged elements, domestic blooms.

SHOE REPAIR

Peter & Sons

peterandsons.com

Three generations of craft began with Peter, who opened the shop in 1980 after immigrating from Ukraine.

GOLF INSTRUCTION

Tommy Cuthbert Golf Center

kiawahresort.com

Video swing analysis, club fitting, practice bunkers and greens, and one-on-one instruction with pros.

INTERIOR DESIGNER

Angie Hranowsky

angiehranowsky.com

Known for her bold mix of vintage and modern. Regularly appears on shelter mags' bests lists.

MARCHING BAND

Burke High School

1burkeband.com

Halftime pomp and swagger with the High Steppin' Bulldog Band.

HOSPITALITY

Steve Palmer

theindigoroad.com

Savvy restaurateur carries the torch for mental health and addiction support in the industry.

BARBER

Broad Street Barber Shop

broadstreetbarbershop.com

The works: hot towel, hot lather, straight-razor shave.

LEATHER GOODS

J. Stark

starkmade.com

Tote everything from toiletries to wine bottles in style.

SOCIAL GOOD

One80 Place

one80place.org

Nonprofit providing food, shelter and support to the houseless.

FOLK ARTIST

P-Nut the Lowcountry Poet

@p_nut_the_legend

With humor and irreverence, Joseph "P-Nut" Johnson captures his hometown.

CREATIVE AGENCY

SDCO Partners

sdcopartners.com

Local clients include Smithey Ironware and Post House Inn.

SOMMELIER

Sarah O'Kelley

grapetotable.com

Head to her high-ceilinged bottle shop for weekly blind tastings and somm school.

PASTRY CHEF

Cynthia Wong

liferafttreats.com

Crafter of ice cream delights in the shape of fried chicken and TV dinner trays.

SELECTED CONTENT

MORE THAN 30 ENTRIES ☞

Excerpts have been edited for clarity and concision.

ALMANAC

A deep dive into the cultural heritage of Charleston through timelines, newspaper clippings, letters, lists and other historical hearsay

THE WALLED CITY

From the 1680s to the 1780s, Charleston was a heavily fortified city, complete with moats, drawbridges, wooden gates with iron-strap hinges, and a medieval-style wall—the better to protect against invaders and pirates. After the Revolutionary War, the wall—the only one of its kind built by the English in America—came down, and people soon forgot it had ever existed. Though most of the thousands of bricks that once made up the perimeter have long since been buried or built over, there are three places where remnants of Charleston's original fortress can still be seen:

1. In the cellar of the Old Exchange Building on Broad Street.

2. In the basement of the Missroon House at 40 East Bay Street, now the headquarters of the Historic Charleston Foundation.

3. On the green at the west end of Marion Square, where a 6-by-6-by-2-foot tabby remnant has been preserved as part of the late-colonial Horn Work Battery.

OPERATION JACKPOT

From 1982 to 1986, a federal drug task force in South Carolina convicted more than 100 "gentlemen smugglers" [so-called for their nonviolent approach] of ferrying hundreds of thousands of pounds of marijuana through the marshes and inlets of the Lowcountry on yachts and fishing vessels. The multi-agency effort, known as Operation Jackpot, became a landmark moment in the '80s-era War on Drugs. Below, a sampling of the busts.

LOCATION	DATE	AMOUNT SEIZED
Great Pee Dee River	Sept '79	34,000 lbs
McClellanville	March '77	22,000 lbs
Seabrook Island	Jan '80	22,000 lbs
Edisto Island	Aug '81	9,800 lbs
Port Royal Sound	June '79	7,000 lbs

PAT CONROY

Master storyteller Pat Conroy was one of the most popular American novelists of the last century. His novels—including The Great Santini, The Lords of Discipline, South of Broad *and* The Prince of Tides*—celebrate the beauty and complexities of the Lowcountry. Conroy lived near Beaufort with his wife, the writer Cassandra King. He passed away in 2016 at the age of 70. Below, an excerpt from* The Prince of Tides.

My wound is geography. It is also my anchorage, my port of call.

I grew up slowly beside the tides and marshes of Colleten; my arms were tawny and strong from working long days on the shrimp boat in the blazing South Carolina heat. Because I was a Wingo, I worked as soon as I could walk; I could pick a blue crab clean when I was five. I had killed my first deer by the age of seven, and at nine was regularly putting meat on my family's table. I was born and raised on a Carolina sea island and I carried the sunshine of the lowcountry, inked in dark gold, on my back and shoulders. As a boy I was happy above the channels, navigating a small boat between the sandbars with their quiet nation of oysters exposed on the brown flats at the low watermark. I knew every shrimper by name, and they knew me and sounded their horns when they passed me fishing in the river.

When I was ten I killed a bald eagle for pleasure, for the singularity of the act, despite the divine, exhilarating beauty of its solitary flight over schools of whiting. It was the only thing I had ever killed that I had never seen before. After my father beat me for breaking the law and for killing the last eagle in Colleton County, he made me build a fire, dress the bird, and eat its flesh as tears rolled down my face. Then he turned me in to Sheriff Benson, who locked me in a cell for over an hour. My father took the feathers and made a crude Indian headdress for me to wear to school. He believed in the expiation of sin. I wore the headdress for weeks, until it began to disintegrate feather by feather. Those feathers trailed me in the hallways of the school as though I were a molting, discredited angel.

"Never kill anything that's rare," my father had said.

"I'm lucky I didn't kill an elephant," I replied.

"You'd have had a mighty square meal if you had," he answered.

My father did not permit crimes against the land. Though I have hunted again, all eagles are safe from me.

THE DART FAMILY

In March 1844, William Dart began a five-year path out of slavery, which culminated in 1849, with his wife, a free woman of color named Susan Fenwick, purchasing his rights. Five years later, they welcomed a son, John Lewis Dart, who would become valedictorian of the Avery Normal Institute's first graduating class, a respected reverend, and a pioneer for Black education in Charleston. Here, two of the legal documents that secured his father's freedom.

For Value Received, I hereby assign, transfer and set over to William B Heriot and his assigns, all my right, title, interest and claim of, in and to the within named Boy William, to have and to hold him, the said Boy William, unto the said William B. Heriot and his assigns, as his and their property forever.

Witness my hand and Seal this 20th of April, 1849.

Robt. Brodie

***

For value received, I hereby assign, transfer and set over unto Susan Fenwick, a free person of Colour, and her assigns, all my right, title, interest and claim of, in and to the within named slave William, to have and to hold him, the said Boy William, unto the said Susan Fenwick and her assigns, as her and their own property forever.

Witness my Hand and Seal this 29 September, 1849.

Williams B. Heriot

The Avery Normal Institute, Charleston's first accredited secondary school for African Americans, was founded in 1865. The Avery Research Center for African American History and Culture is now located at the site.

WALKING TOUR

A selection of off-the-record stops for roaming the historic peninsula.

COOPER-O'CONNOR HOUSE

180 *Broad St*

Used as a prison for Union officers during the Civil War. Left untouched by Union artillery during the Union bombardment.

JOHNSON-POINSETT TENEMENT

22-24 *State St*

Though you could easily miss it if you were not looking for it, the shape of a phallus outlines the doorway to this former brothel.

MCKINLAY BUILDING

139 *Market St*

In 1927, two gunmen shot Irish gangster Rumpty Rattles from the second story windows. Rattles was unarmed and shot in the back, but the killers were acquitted on self-defense.

DR. JOSEPH JOHNSON HOUSE

56 *Society St*

The 1960s home of English author Dawn Langley Simmons and husband John-Paul Simmons. Theirs was the first legal interracial marriage in Charleston.

ABBOTT MIDDLETON HOUSE

48 *Murray Blvd*

Rear garage apartment was home to a young John Fitzgerald Kennedy, who was stationed in Charleston with the Navy during World War II.

GRACE PEIXOTTO HOUSE

11 *Fulton St*

The brothel of the most famous madam in Charleston's history. Peixotto's funeral was rumored to boast South Carolina's longest-ever procession.

ORANGE STREET

Cut down the east edge of the Orange Garden just prior to the Revolution. Said to have been a meeting site for one of the first pleasure cults in America.

THOMAS ROSE HOUSE

59 *Church St*

In 1786, Dr. Joseph Brown Ladd, defending the honor of a local actress, was shot in a duel and later succumbed to his wound in this nearby boarding house. His ghost is rumored to haunt the street.

HURRICANE HUGO

In 1989, this brief but powerful storm cut a path of destruction from the Caribbean to the Appalachians, killing more than 80 people and resulting in $17.4 billion in damages.

Sept 11	Tropical Storm Hugo forms in Atlantic Ocean
Sept 15	Hugo upgraded to Category 4 hurricane
Sept 17	Hugo hits Lesser Antilles' Leeward Islands, 21 dead
Sept 18	South Carolina Governor Carroll Campbell briefed on emergency procedures
Sept 19	Hugo pounds Puerto Rico with 125 mile per hour winds
Sept 20	Voluntary evacuation begins along South Carolina coast
	Police stow chainsaws, bulldozers across Charleston
	State of emergency declared, 7 p.m.
Sept 21	Barrier islands ordered to evacuate, 7 a.m.
	Traffic jam forms on I-26, then inexplicably clears, 8 a.m.
	Hurricane-force winds hit the Battery, 11:30 p.m.
	MUSC Hospital maintenance workers tie themselves to a fuel pump to keep emergency generator running
Sept 22	Hugo makes landfall, 12 a.m.
	Eye of the storm passes over Charleston, 12:30 a.m.
	Folly Beach's famous Atlantic House restaurant destroyed; 30 to 80 percent of local homes uninhabitable
	750,000 South Carolinians without power
Sept 23	Some 56,000 Lowcountry residents homeless
	Sewer systems down. Drinking water scarce.
	Charleston Mayor Joe Riley instates 7 p.m. to 7 a.m. curfew
	Isle of Palms Mayor Carmen Bunch declares martial law
	National Guard troops arrive on Sullivan's Island
Sept 25	Another storm dumps rain on the Lowcountry. Floodwaters rise. Cleanup and recovery efforts stall.
	Hugo dissipates over Atlantic Ocean

CHEF NAT FULLER

Nat Fuller, one of the most respected chefs and caterers in Charleston in the 1850s and '60s, was also enslaved. Working under the "self-hire" system [where slaves with certain transferable skills would pay a portion of their earnings to their captors in exchange for greater autonomy], Fuller opened his restaurant, The Bachelor's Retreat, in October 1860, on the corner of Church Street and Saint Michael's Alley. Fuller advertised it as "a favorite resort for gentlemen who desire lunches, meals or refreshments at any hours." In the spring of 1865, now a free man, Nat Fuller hosted perhaps the most famous dinner in the city's history, a "miscegenation feast" that brought whites and Blacks to shared tables in celebration of Lincoln, emancipation and the end of the Civil War.

BEACH MUSIC

Around 1945, *a new kind of sound began cropping up along ocean drives throughout the Lowcountry. Beach music, as it came to be called, borrowed its soul from Motown and its dance-friendly rhythms from the blues. For a history lesson in song, listen to these timeless hits.*

FIRST WAVE 1945–1954	"Sixty Minute Man" by Billy Ward and the Dominoes "Money Honey" by Clyde McPhatter and the Drifters
SECOND WAVE 1955–1961	"Stagger Lee" by Lloyd Price "Stay" by Maurice Williams and the Zodiacs
THIRD WAVE 1962–1970	"39-21-40 Shape" by The Showmen "With this Ring" by The Platters
FOURTH WAVE 1971–1979	"Summertime's Calling Me" by The Catalinas "I Love Beach Music" by The Embers
FIFTH WAVE *Early* 1980s	"Carolina Girls" by General Johnson "Myrtle Beach Days" by Fantastic Shakers

BOTANY OF NOTE

PLANT	DESCRIPTION
Aster	*Autumn favorites with stars of white, lavender, pink or purple petals*
Azaleas	*Garden mainstays in full bloom just in time for Masters golf*
Bald Cypress	*Knobby-kneed trees buttress themselves in swampy, humid environs*
Bergamot	*Eye candy for hummingbirds and butterflies, citrusy glamour for hot-tea drinkers*
Camellia	*This showy evergreen is a welcome sight in the dead of winter*
Carolina Indigo	*Old-world cash crop currently making a violet-hued comeback*
Cotton Rose	*Deceptively named hibiscus with color-changing tendencies*
Crape Myrtle	*Multi-branched shrubs shake crinkly-bloom fists at the summer swelter*
Gardenia	*Intoxicatingly fragrant white blossoms with trademark waxy leaves*
Live Oak	*Old-growth trees with evergreen leaves and majestic canopies*
Noisette Rose	*Charleston-specific hybrid blooms from spring to fall*
Palmetto Tree	*Thatched-trunk trees, top-heavy tufts of spiky leaves*
Magnolia	*Three species do well in Charleston, but Bull Bay is the favorite*
Spanish Moss	*Ethereal, gray, rootless ghosts hang on elder oaks*
Yellow Jessamine	*Fragrant climbers, trumpet-shaped yellow flowers*
Wisteria	*Billowing lilac flowers top old-town pergolas and historic dividing walls*

Aster

Yellow Jessamine

Magnolia

Noisette Rose

SHEPARD FAIREY

Charleston native Shepard Fairey is one of the world's most influential and well-known artists. Born in 1970, Fairey attended Wando High School before going on to California's Idyllwild Arts Academy and the Rhode Island School of Design. At RISD, Fairey created "Andre the Giant Has A Posse," a sticker campaign that would grow to achieve international levels of exposure. In 2008, Fairey created the "Hope" stencil poster, depicting then-presidential candidate Barack Obama, which art critic Peter Schjeldahl called "the most efficacious American political illustration since 'Uncle Sam Wants You.'" The National Portrait Gallery in Washington, D.C., acquired the original in 2009. Today, the best spot to see Shepherd Fairey's local marks is the large-scale *Power & Glory* mural on upper King outside Butcher & Bee restaurant.

GARDEN & GUN

Charleston-based lifestyle magazine *Garden & Gun* launched in 2007, hitting newsstands during a blistering recession that toppled many of its brethren—*Gourmet, Southern Accents, Condé Nast Portfolio.* The inaugural issue had a distribution of 150,000 copies and featured a barefooted Pat Conroy on its cover. As of 2021, its more than 1.6 million readers include residents of all 50 states, as well as a strong following abroad. The name, perhaps the most common inquiry about the magazine, is both a metaphor for the confluence of land and culture, and a nod to the King Street Garden and Gun Club, a now-shuttered nightclub first located at 240 King Street and later in a warehouse on the west side of Church Street, where Hank's Seafood now stands. Founded by Richard Robison, one of the Spoleto Festival producers, the Garden and Gun Club opened in 1976 to give artists and performers a late-night joint for post-festival revelry, and the spot rattled on in business until late 1981. While no trace of the disco remains in Charleston, the original spirit of progressive Southern thought [and a fondness for whiskey] endures inside each issue of the magazine.

PAINT COLORS

The Historic Charleston Foundation's official Lowcountry palette, by landscape.

MARSH

Pluff Mud [brown]
Windmill Rose [yellow]
Wadmalaw Green [gray-green]
Ferry Blue [ocean green]
Bohicket Thistle [eggplant]
Gullah Blue [turquoise]

ISLAND

Creek Shrimp [light pink]
Stained Boards [taupe]
Shoreline [white-gray]
Noon Sky [baby blue]
Summer Linen [off-white]
Beach Flower [coral]

VILLAGE

Tin Roof [dark gray]
Alhambra Blue [blue-green]
Grocery Store Red [brick]
Chain Stitch [light purple]
Village Porch [salmon]
Chapel of Ease [white]

EDGAR ALLAN POE

Edgar Allan Poe's short story "The Gold-Bug," published in 1843, takes place on Sullivan's Island, where he lived for a short time. Today, the island library and a local tavern carry the writer's name. Below, a short excerpt from the story.

This Island is a very singular one. It consists of little else than the sea sand, and is about three miles long. Its breadth at no point exceeds a quarter of a mile. It is separated from the mainland by a scarcely perceptible creek, oozing its way through a wilderness of reeds and slime, a favorite resort of the marsh-hen. The vegetation, as might be supposed, is scant, or at least dwarfish. No trees of any magnitude are to be seen. Near the western extremity, where Fort Moultrie stands, and where are some miserable frame buildings, tenanted, during summer, by the fugitives from Charleston dust and fever, may be found, indeed, the bristly palmetto; but the whole island, with the exception of this western point, and a line of hard, white beach on the sea-coast, is covered with a dense undergrowth of the sweet myrtle, so much prized by the horticulturists of England.

PLUFF MUD

Scientific American: Volume 23, 1887

"IMMEDIATELY BENEATH THE SOIL IN THE LOW GROUNDS OCCURS A BED OF FINE CLAYEY SAND OR SILT, GENERALLY BLUISH IN COLOR. THIS STRATUM COMMONLY CONTAINS SULPHURETS AND VARIOUS SALTS, EITHER FREE OR QUICKLY LIBERATED ON OXIDATION. IT IS FROM TEN TO THIRTY OR FORTY FEET THICK; THE PRECISE THICKNESS BEING DIFFICULT TO DETERMINE, PARTLY BECAUSE OF THE LOCAL THICKENING DUE TO DEPRESSIONS IN THE SUBJACENT SURFACE, AND PARTLY BECAUSE OF THE IMPOSSIBILITY OF SEPARATING IT FROM THE SUPERJACENT MEMBER. … IN THE LOW GROUNDS, AND ALONG THE COAST GENERALLY, THESE SANDS ARE OVERLAIN OR REPLACED BY ESTUARINE ALLUVIUM CONSISTING OF FINE BLUE SILT OR CLAY, LOCALLY DESIGNATED "PLUFF MUD;" FOR THE SAND IS NOW SUBSIDING [AND APPARENTLY MOST RAPIDLY SOUTHWESTWARD], AND SEDIMENTATION IS ADVANCING UPON THE LAND. BENEATH THESE SUPERFICIAL DEPOSITS OCCURS THE COMMONLY RECOGNIZED "MARL BED," AT THE SUMMIT OF WHICH THE SOUTH CAROLINA PHOSPHATES ARE FOUND. … THESE FORMATIONS CONSIST OF A SOMEWHAT VARIABLE BUT NEVERTHELESS REMARKABLY UNIFORM SUCCESSION OF MARLS, CLAYS, AND SANDS, EXTENDING TO A DEPTH OF ABOUT SIX HUNDRED FEET, WHERE THEY ARE UNDERLAIN BY PETROGRAPHICALLY SIMILAR CRETACEOUS DEPOSITS, INCREASING IN HETEROGENEITY SOMEWHAT DOWNWARD TO TWO THOUSAND FEET BELOW THE SURFACE. AT THIS DEPTH A GOOD SUPPLY OF ARTESIAN WATER HAS BEEN OBTAINED."

Translation: When the Lowcountry's marshland melting pot of decaying crustaceans, decomposing plants, dead amoebae, waterfowl droppings, Spartina grass, snails, saltwater and mudflats is exposed at low tide, it releases hydrogen sulfide [a.k.a. the good-bad smell of home].

ALLEYS OF NOTE

CHALMERS STREET
Located in the French Quarter between State and Meeting streets, Charleston's longest remaining cobblestone street is named for Dr. Lionel Chalmers, who purchased property there in 1757. In between his pioneering work studying tetanus and fevers, Chalmers dabbled in meteorology.

LAMBOLL STREET
Throughout its history, Lamboll has been called Smith Lane, Dedcott's Alley, Rivers Street and Kincaid Street, after various property owners. Its present name comes from Thomas Lamboll, an 18th-century botanist and rose enthusiast whose even greater legacy is White Point Garden.

PHILADELPHIA ALLEY
In 1810, William Johnson, who owned much of the property around Kinloch Court, petitioned city officials to rename the small passageway in unlikely homage to the City of Brotherly Love, where he was imprisoned during the Revolutionary War. Today, it connects Queen and Cumberland streets.

STOLL'S ALLEY
Just 17 bricks wide at its entrance on East Bay Street, Stoll's Alley is named for 18th-century blacksmith Justinus Stoll, who built his home there in 1745.

UNITY ALLEY
Running between East Bay and State streets, this narrow passage has long been a favorite among locals looking to indulge. In 1775 the first tavern set up shop; today, its most famous resident is McCrady's restaurant.

ROPEMAKERS LANE
The site of Charles Snetter's rope manufactory from the 1790s until 1803, this 100-foot straightaway just off lower Meeting Street was originally used for laying out and twisting lengths of rope by hand.

LONGITUDE LANE
A preserved country lane smack in the middle of downtown, Longitude offers a time-capsule look at life in the 1600s. Its sidewalls and trees are a popular spot for name-carving.

SHIPWRECKS

Since the 16th century, countless ships have ventured into the waters off the 211 miles of South Carolina coastline. These unlucky vessels didn't survive the trip.

Capitana 1526	Lost near present-day Georgetown in a failed attempt by the Spanish to establish the first European settlement on the North American mainland.
Queen of France 1779	Earliest U.S. Navy vessel to go down off the South Carolina coast was purposely sunk in Charleston Harbor to block British ships from entering.
General Hodgkinson 1813	This ship from Curaçao met its end near Charleston. Local treasure hunters have long claimed it could contain millions in gold or currency.
SS Central America 1857	Sank en route to New York in September. Loss of 30,000 pounds of gold contributed to the Panic of 1857. More than $200 million worth has been reclaimed.
CSS Georgiana 1863	Scuttled off Isle of Palms after being damaged in battle. Located in 1965; salvage operation found historic items, but not the rumored cache of gold.
H.L. Hunley 1863	Sank after torpedoing the Union Army's *Housatonic*. Novelist Clive Cussler located the remains off the coast of Sullivan's Island in 1995.

CIVIL WAR

John's Island
August 21, 1864

Last night at 9 o'clock I burnt Legareville. The buildings were at almost the same instant set on fire and were in a few minutes a sheet of flames. The battery on Horse Island fired a farewell shot into the picket house before we had left. After a considerable time the battery and gunboat renewed their fire, throwing their shell into the villages and up the peninsula upon which Legareville stood to Bryan's place, a distance of 3 miles. Some 15 or 20 shots were fired, from which we sustained no injury. When the determination to destroy the village was announced the Stono Scouts, owners of the property on the place, volunteered to aid the detachment from Captain Clark's company ordered for the purpose, 16 such members applying the torches to their own dwellings. To-day, after 16 months' duty on this outpost, I turn over the command to Captain Parker, and report to my regiment with regret that my last official act on the island should have been, under an imperative sense of duty, to recommend the destruction of the property ... and assisting with my own hands in applying the torch to their dwellings. I am only reconciled by reflection that the property had served useful ends to the enemy, who were removing it for their accommodation to the islands in their possession, and it would have been in any event lost to the owners. Five schooners, 2 brigs, and 1 gun-boat in the Stono and Folly Rivers; 1 gun-boat in the North Edisto River.

John Jenkins
Major, Commanding
3rd South Carolina Cavalry

Libraries could be filled with books about the Civil War, and Charleston plays a central role in each of them. A recent standout is Our Man in Charleston: Britain's Secret Agent in the Civil War South *by Christopher Dickey, which tracks the double life of Robert Bunch, an abolitionist spy from London who rubbed shoulders with Holy City elite throughout the war years, endeavoring to thwart Confederate aims.*

SEPTIMA POINSETTE CLARK

Born in Charleston in 1898, Septima Clark was a legendary figure in civil rights, called the "Mother of the Movement" by Martin Luther King Jr. For more than half a century, Clark focused her energies on education equality, teaching rural students on Johns Island [sometimes more than 100 to a classroom], as well as establishing a network of "Citizenship Schools" that specialized in teaching uneducated adults across the Deep South how to read. Clark was also the first female board member of the highly influential Southern Christian Leadership Conference. The below excerpt is taken from an interview with Clark about her mother and growing up in turn-of-the-century Charleston.

Interviewed by Jacquelyn Dowd Hall

JULY 25, 1976

CLARK: In the days when segregation was very great, [my mother] had courage enough to speak against it to us. We lived on a street that was integrated, and there was an Irishman down the street who didn't want you to skate in front of his door. And so she would always have something to say about it.

HALL: Did she speak to him?

SPC: Right out to him.

JDH: What would she say?

SPC: Just tell him that the street didn't belong to him. He said, "Well, I paid for it in front of my door." But she said, "That doesn't allow you to tell these children they can't skate past that door." But we were afraid of him, and when we got to his door, we'd always slide around into the street and go on.

[*Laughter*]

JDH: Was it common for the streets to be integrated ...

SPC: At that time. Yes.

JDH: When you were growing up?

SPC: We had Italians and Irish on the same street, and Germans, all living in between.

JDH: Did the children play with each other? Did black and white children play together?

SPC: No, unh-uh, as a rule they didn't. When the black children were out in the street playing, all of the whites or the others would be in their homes. And whenever the white children came out, why, the parents kept you away from them, too.

JDH: Did your mother have any good relationships with her white neighbors, any friendly relationships with the whites and the blacks?

SPC: I couldn't say yes. I don't know if she had any. My father would speak to everyone, but my mother wouldn't. And there was a group of—I guess they were either Germans and Irish—across from [us] and they had a car out in the street and they sold this bootleg. They would come sit on our step, you know, and when people'd come up you see them going into this car, you know, selling the bootleg liquor ... I didn't really know what they were doing at that time. But my mother didn't want them to sit on her step. I guess she understood what they were doing. And she would lock the door and then take some water and throw it under the door, and they couldn't understand where this water was coming from. That's the way she did.

JDH: You mean she would wet the steps and then go inside and lock the door?

SPC: No.

JDH: She'd throw it down?

SPC: Throw it underneath the door.

JDH: Oh, under the door.

SPC: Yes. Throw it very quietly. Yes. They'd be getting up and looking, wondering where this water was coming from.

JDH: Amazing.

Courtesy of the Southern Oral History Collection at the University of North Carolina at Chapel Hill.

THE HOLY CITY

Every hour, throughout the day, the sound of church bells—some of which are more than 250 years old—ring out across the peninsula. The source? A handful of historic churches whose dedicated local ringers carry on a musical tradition that dates back to 17th-century England. *Change ringing* relies on an interconnected network of bells [usually somewhere between eight and 10] to produce different sounds. And since each bell is attached to its own wheel, which rotates with a simple hand-pull, a single person of any age can deftly maneuver each instrument, some of which exceed 1,600 pounds. Throug-out Charleston's history, church bells have been used to announce births and deaths, call people to worship, even alert residents of fire, storms and approaching enemies. So when you hear something that sounds more urgent than your average chime, you can bet that the ringers in one of these four belfries know something you don't.

THE CATHEDRAL CHURCH OF ST. LUKE AND ST. PAUL
126 *Coming St*
Eight bells, including six cast in the 1880s

GRACE CHURCH CATHEDRAL
98 *Wentworth St*
Ten bells, including eight circa-1883 heirlooms transplanted from a shuttered church in England

ST. MICHAEL'S CHURCH
71 *Broad St*
Eight bells originally cast in 1764

STELLA MARIS CATHOLIC CHURCH
1204 *Middle St, Sullivan's Island*
Eight bells—the first Roman Catholic church in the country to have a set

HERITAGE CROPS

A farmer's market shopping list of bygone ingredients saved from extinction.

Carolina African runner peanut
The first peanut cultivated in North America—an import brought by enslaved Africans. Harvested in 2013 for the first time in half a century.

Palmetto asparagus
Once the most famous asparagus in the country, now maintained by a small but growing number of South Carolina farmers.

Sapelo Island sugar cane
A group of sea islanders is reintroducing the hardy purple ribbon strain, not grown here commercially in a hundred years.

Carolina Gold rice
The grandfather of native long-grain rice was one of the first heirloom ingredients to be restored to glory.

Sea Island red peas
These heirloom field peas were used in the earliest versions of Hoppin' John in the 17th century.

Purple cape beans
Nineteenth-century Cape Romain fishermen loved these recently reintroduced miniature kidney-shaped beans.

Benne
The revived ancestor of the sesame seed underpinned countless Lowcountry dishes until industrial strains took over in the 1940s.

Henry Moore yellow hominy corn
Native hominy corn has been bred for over 150 years and is still milled the old-fashioned way.

Red May wheat
Prized for its hardiness and flavor, this preindustrial grain has survived drought and disease, and thrives in hot climates.

Abruzzi rye
A spicy, nutty heirloom famous during the colonial era, Abruzzi is gaining newfound traction among bakers.

French peelcorn oats
New crop oats cultivated from ancient seeds are still hand-harvested by coastal farmers.

THE GREAT EARTHQUAKE

September 1, 1886
3 a.m.

My dear Mr. Horn:

We have all gone through a fearful ordeal, but thank God we all live. A terrible earthquake. We had just had prayers, 9:30 p.m., and in less than 6 minutes the house commenced to rock and furniture and all small articles thrown about. ... All gas light went out. I did not know how soon the house would be down on us. At first cessation I lit my lamp to see after the children. Your wardrobe had fallen on Chisholm's and Willie's bed. Chisholm was covered in some kind of medicine from your wardrobe, but thank God not one of them with a scratch.

I am satisfied there is not a family tonight but what are out in the street. All on the Mill lot, white and black, old and young, gathered by the croquet ground, and there we have been ever since. ... I am afraid the damages are infinitely worse than from the cyclone. ... I am afraid there is much loss of life. Numbers of ladies rushing out of the houses with simply night dress. No time to put on anything. ... It will be some time before we can rest quietly after this terrible experience.

I understand part of the *News & Courier* office is down, so I may not be able to send you a copy of the paper. Police station portico fell, but I hear no one hurt. Indeed the city must look worse than it did after the cyclone and much more danger from the cracked walls. ... Just after the shock there was a fearfully strong smell of mud, such as I have experienced in Stono River when the tube was sunk to bring up mud that had lain there undisturbed for centuries perhaps. And I presume the earth had affected the bottom of the river here so as to bring this stuff to the surface. It was high tide at the time—9 o'clock.

Now it is 4 a.m. ... The children are all asleep in the office. ... The Alstons came down to the Mill about 2 a.m. to see how we fared. They are all on Cantini lot, foot of Savage St. No one indoors anywhere I think tonight.

Much love from all.
Yours affectionately,
Robert G. Chisholm

NAUTICAL KNOTS

Familiarize yourself with a handful of basic ties, and you'll be primed to navigate both open sea and backwater.

BOWLINE

Used to form a fixed loop at the end of a rope. Common when sailing small craft. Sometimes called the "king of knots."

FIGURE EIGHT

One of the strongest sailing knots. Like the bowline, made at the end of a line. Also known as the Flemish knot.

CARRICK BEND

An over-under basket-weave knot used for joining two lines of heavy rope or cable. Alternate name: the sailor's breastplate.

SHEET BEND

Used to join two ropes of unequal thickness. Knot most often used in net-making.

ROLLING HITCH

Will keep any line affixed to a vertical object like a post. Also key for securing tent pegs and awnings.

CLEAT HITCH

The standard way to tether a boat to a dock cleat. Relies on a simple figure-eight loop that pins the free end under the last wrap.

MARLINGSPIKE HITCH

Quick way of gripping a pole or a bar when you need it to take weight, making it ideal for ladder-making.

DOUBLE BLACKWALL HITCH

A temporary means of securing a line to a cargo hook. More secure than the standard blackwall hitch.

Boating knots typically fall into three categories: knots, which are made at the end of a rope; bends, which are generally used to connect two separate pieces of rope or line; and hitches, which secure a line to a cleat or similar stationary post.

PRAISE HOUSES

Built circa 1917, the Moving Star Hall on Johns Island is the only remaining praise house of the South Carolina sea islands to have been identified. Though tiny, it has always been big on spirited songs, many of which are done as a call and response, with a song leader carrying the verses and the congregation repeating back the hymn's refrain.

MRS. BERTHA SMITH AND THE MOVING STAR CONGREGATION'S "LAY DOWN BODY"

Leader: I know you tired,
Group: Lay down a little while,
Leader: I know you tired,
Group: Lay down a little while.

Verse 2: Come from a distance ...
Verse 3: Oh body now ...
Verse 4: Ain't you had a hard time? ...
Verse 5: Last December ...
Verse 6: Tedious was my journey ...
Verse 7: Rocky was my road, Lord ...
Verse 8: Ain't you got somebody gone? ...
Verse 9: I got somebody gone ...
Verse 10: Oh my body now ...
Verse 11: Just keep a-rollin' ...
Verse 12: Body, ain't you tired? ...
Verse 13: Body, ain't you lonesome? ...
Verse 14: Body, ain't you weary? ...

All: Lay down body,
Lay down a little while,
Lay down body,
Lay down a little while.

MELLICHAMP AND MUIR

Martinez, California.
October 15, 1901.

My dear Dr. Mellichamp,

Many thanks for the fine sets of specimens of P. Cubensis and Q. Myrtifolia, all of which came to hand in excellent order.

I had not before noticed that this or indeed any of our oaks matured at once both annual & biennial fruits, but I see that Prof. Sargent in a note gives you credit for this discovery in his Silva.

I'm glad you liked my tribute to Joseph LeConte & got pleasure from it. He who had the same peculiar charming southern manners & was greatly admired & loved by those who got near him seems to be almost forgotten by the world at large.

I am sending with this a sketch of the Glaciers of the coast, which I wrote for the first of the Harrman Ixpedition [sic] books, & of which the publisher sent me a few extra copies. Unfortunately the best of the illustrations of the Muir Glacier are in other parts of the book—a big 2 vol. affair gotten up in grand style, but I may get them for you yet. How vast and wild our country still is! & how strange these icy parts must seem to a Southern Carolinian.

With hearty thanks, my dear Dr. I am faithfully yours

Signed John Muir.

Dr. Joseph H. Mellichamp was a beloved physician and lifelong student of Southern flora, corresponding with many of the preeminent botanists of his era, including John Muir, and freely sharing hundreds of Lowcountry specimens. Dr. Mellichamp died in November 1903 on James Island, where he was raised.

THE CHURCH AND THE TIDES

"Before the Huguenot settlers living up the Cooper and Santee Rivers had their own churches, they came to town for services at the Huguenot Church, [on the] corner of Church and Queen streets. The only road into town was a very long and roundabout way from their settlements, besides being dangerous because of possible attack by Indians, and also because of the natural hazards of a trip through wild, unsettled country. Therefore they came to town by water—in canoes, or in periaugers [a kind of canoe dug out of a single huge log]. These craft were difficult to manage against tide, especially when loaded with passengers. So, the settlers would wait for an ebb-tide to float down with it to services, then make the return trip on the flood-tide. And the Church timed its services accordingly."

Excerpted from official Lectures for Guides,
collected in 1964 by Elizabeth Stallworth.

SPOLETO

Spoleto is an annual celebration of artistic performance, spanning experimental to established works, held every spring. Since its beginning in 1977, Spoleto has played host to numerous world premieres, including:

1978: *Creve Coeur,* Tennessee Williams .... Theater
1980: *The American Clock,* Arthur Miller .... Theater
1984: *Spoleto Express Breakdancers,* Julie Arenal .... Dance
1989: *Empty Places,* Laurie Anderson .... Opera
1989: *Wall Drawings,* Sol LeWitt .... Visual Art
1990: *Hydrogen Jukebox,* Philip Glass and Allen Ginsberg .... Opera
1991: *The Mysteries and What's So Funny?,*
David Gordon and Philip Glass .... Musical Theater
1991: *Wall, Soaring, Ground Level, Impact,* Elizabeth Streb .... Dance
1991: *Places with a Past: New Site-Specific Art in Charleston,* Mary Jane Jacob .... Visual Art
1993: *The Singing Child,* Gian Carlo Menotti .... Opera
1996: *Peter and Wendy,* Lee Breuer and Liza Lorwin,
adapted from the novel by J.M. Barrie .... Musical Theater

RICE PILAU

When *The Carolina Housewife by a Lady of Charleston* was published in 1847, it didn't take long for locals to identify Sarah "Sally" Rutledge, the daughter of a signer of the Declaration of Independence, as the cookbook's anonymous author. Today, Rutledge's text endures as an indispensable guide to Lowcountry—and Southern—cuisine, thanks to its gone-era know-how ["Kill whatever you wish to dress the evening before, and throw it immediately into cold water"] and Rutledge's uncannily prescient curation of dishes that were, even then, on their way to becoming regional classics. Her rice pilau is a Charleston signature, and recalls a time when it wasn't uncommon for locals to eat some form of the grain three times a day. Below, Sally's word-for-word instructions on preparing the dish.

Boil one and a half pounds of bacon. When nearly done, throw into the pot a quart of rice, which must be first washed and graveled. Then put in the fowls [one or two, according to size], and season with pepper and salt. In serving up, which should be done as soon as possible after the fowls are cooked enough, put the rice first in the dish, and the bacon and fowls upon it.

MRS. SMITH'S SHRIMP CASSEROLE

This recipe for shrimp and red-rice casserole, recovered from a circa-1911 house on Meeting Street several decades later, was handwritten on a piece of monogrammed stationery.

Cook two cups white rice. Meanwhile, melt one stick of butter in a cast-iron skillet. Add one large chopped onion and one hot pepper and cook until tender. Add one can tomato sauce and three pounds cooked shrimp. Season with salt, pepper, and Worcestershire sauce to taste. Pour in casserole dish along with cooked rice and bake for twenty minutes in a 350 degree oven.

HISTORIC AMERICAN FIRSTS IN CHARLESTON

A short list of pioneering moves.

PUBLIC LIBRARY	1700
FEMALE ARTIST	1707
THEATER	1736
WEATHERMAN	1737
PUBLIC MUSEUM	1773
BLACK BAPTIST CHURCH	1773
CHAMBER OF COMMERCE	1773
AMERICAN ARCHITECT	1781
GOLF CLUB	1786
COMMERCIAL ICE BUSINESS	1799
REFORM JEWISH CONGREGATION	1824
PASSENGER RAILROAD SERVICE	1830
CITY COLLEGE	1836

TEA AND COFFEE

In lean times, when the residents of Charleston's nearby sea islands didn't have the means or access to buy tea and coffee, they improvised recipes for their daily brew.

GRITS TEA

Put grits in a frying pan on the fire and let them parch until brown. Then, pour water in the pan, steep and strain.

CORN COFFEE

Remove kernels from a cob of corn and sear. Meanwhile, boil a pot of water. When the corn is nearly burned, drop it into the pot of boiling water. Steep and strain.

LONESOMEST MAN IN TOWN

Collier's magazine, April 29, 1950

by Samuel Grafton

AN IMPRESSIVE six-footer, of humor and charm, Federal Judge J. Waties Waring, of Charleston, South Carolina, has unimpeachable social background and high standing in the law—but almost no white person in Charleston will call on him or, if he can help it, speak to him.

Elderly gentlewomen, forgetting their dignity, whip around street corners when the judge or Mrs. Waring approaches. Men the judge has know since school days, and he is sixty-nine, turn aside and manifest deep interest in the window display of, say a cleaning and dyeing establishment or an emporium selling baby shoes, until he passes by.

The old prep-school business of sending a man "to Coventry," of refusing to speak to him, of looking through him, and carrying on, in general, as if he were not there, is being re-enacted in Charleston, with a federal judge as the object.

J. Waties Waring is, of course, the judge who ruled, in a vigorous and since famous 1947 opinion, that Negroes must be given the full right to vote in South Carolina's [previously] all-white Democratic primaries. Thirty-five thousand Negroes went to the primary polls the following year for the first time, and white Charleston stopped coming to the judge's house.

At least that's the way I had heard it. A sad and simple story, of an angry city and a lonely man. A story that, in its essentials, I could have written without leaving my Connecticut acres. But in Charleston I learned something of what makes men and cities act and react on each other in ways that cannot be summed up in a sentence.

The boycott against Judge Waring is complete. He has

resigned from his local clubs, societies and trusteeships. "A stone wall of unpleasantness," as he puts it, met him wherever he went, and he had to send in those little notes, withdrawing from associations that the better part of eight generations of Warings had belonged to. There are stores with which he has had to stop trading. One of the Charleston guidebooks mentions the unusual fan window above the doorway on his wide, handsome gray house on Meeting Street, but the judge no longer expects white Charleston to knock on the door beneath it.

So deep does feeling run that in the last Democratic primary election, the famous balloting of '48, in which Negroes voted for the first time, all five of the senatorial candidates campaigned very largely on the ground of their disapproval of Judge Waring, giving the new Negro voters a somewhat limited choice. Recently, impeachment petitions against the judge have been circulated, hand to hand, in several parts of the state. And, just a few weeks ago, a flaming cross burned near his home.

All this has happened to Judge Waring in his late sixties, with no sign in the first six and one-half decades of his life that it was destined for so strange an evening.

One talks with Charleston, and the picture that emerges is of a well-regarded local lawyer, J. Waties Waring, "a rather plodding lawyer, in fact," who worked his way along for 40 years in a sober business practice, becoming corporation counsel of the city of Charleston for a time, and then, in 1942, being made federal judge, to universal approval. A well-qualified, unexciting man.

And then suddenly: "—Why he'd never shown any interest in the Negroes before," says one man bitterly. "Then he writes this decision, full of insults to the South. He says it is time for South Carolina to 'rejoin the Union,' and so forth. It wasn't only the decision that made people angry. It was the way he did it. Something come over him."

Judge J. Waties Waring left Charleston in 1952, following another controversial case, Briggs vs. Elliott, *that pushed for desegregation of public schools. He died in New York City in* 1968. *Forty-seven years later, in the summer of 2015, the federal courthouse on Meeting Street was renamed for him.*

MOTHER EMANUEL: A REMEMBRANCE

Emanuel African Methodist Episcopal Church is the oldest AME church in the South and a cornerstone of African American life in Charleston. On July 17, 2015, a white supremacist shot and killed nine members inside the church: Cynthia Hurd, Susie Jackson, Ethel Lance, DePayne Middleton Doctor, Clementa Pinckney, Tywanza Sanders, Daniel Lee Simmons Sr., Sharonda Singleton and Myra Thompson. Below, selections from The Post and Courier*'s remembrance of the victims.*

ETHEL LANCE

Everyone who knew Ethel Lance described her as a joy to be around. But she also had to deal with many heartaches in her lifetime. Her husband, Nathaniel Lance, died in 1988. And she cared for one of her three daughters, Terrie Washington, who was battling cancer before the disease claimed her daughter's life in 2013. To help her through those troubling times, Lance often sang "One Day At a Time," a gospel song about facing life's daily challenges with strength and faith. "One day at a time, sweet Jesus, " the song goes, "That's all I'm asking of you, just give me the strength to do every day what I have to do." Nadine Collier, one of Lance's daughters, said her mother would sing that song every Wednesday on senior citizen night for others in the church group at Mother Emanuel AME. "The people would say, 'Go ahead Ethel, even though you can't sing the thing, we going to sit here and listen to you, so you go ahead and sing your song' and they would laugh and all," Collier said. "But that was her favorite song. ... That song just does something for her." Many times, Lance would sing it through her tears, as she mourned the loss of her daughter. "That song just gives her strength, to keep on and moving on, because she could only do things one day at a time," Collier said. "She went through a lot." Now, Collier said, her mother's favorite song might provide some solace to the rest of the community, as many in Charleston grapple to understand the tragedy. —*Written by Abigail Darlington*

DANIEL L. SIMMONS SR.

Simmons was a gentle man with an easy smile. He was born 74 years ago just as the country was about to endure its Second World War. Simmons would go on to fight in another war, Vietnam, and return with a Purple Heart. Later, he found himself called to a different form of service, the ministry. ... "Dependable, that's how I would describe him, and an excellent administrator," said the Rev. Joe Darby, presiding elder of the church's Beaufort District. "And he had a very good sense of humor." Humor is an important endurance food for any minister. After about 30 years as a pastor, Simmons retired, but as Darby said, "ministers never really retire." Simmons soon joined the ministerial staff of Mother Emanuel, the AME church's spiritual heart. Simmons was the only victim to survive the gunfire. An ambulance rushed him to Medical University Hospital. An emergency team worked on him into early morning, until he could endure no more. But endurance comes in many forms. In Simmons' case, this includes his family. In the aftermath, his son would cite Romans 15:5 and "the God who gives the power of patient endurance." And his granddaughter would face the young man charged with nine counts of murder, now shackled: "Everyone's plea for your soul is proof they lived in love and their legacies will live in love." —*Written by Tony Bartelme*

MYRA THOMPSON

A few years back, members of Emanuel AME Church gathered along Rutledge Avenue to mark the renovation of their vacant parsonage, which had been rescued from a state of crumbling disrepair. ... A devout woman with a clear sense of purpose, Thompson had been the perfect choice to lead the church's property committee. She and her pastor, Clementa Pinckney, shared a passion for restoring and preserving Emanuel's historic buildings, helping a church that had survived fire, an earthquake and racial strife prosper into the future. ... The 59-year-old mother and pastor's wife decided more than a year ago to heed an even deeper calling within the church—to join the ministry. As she had with the property committee, she put her full effort into the pursuit. Thompson received her license to the ministry Wednesday night. A short time later she was dead, gunned down by a young man who she and her friends had welcomed into their house of faith. —*Written by Glenn Smith*

INCLUDED

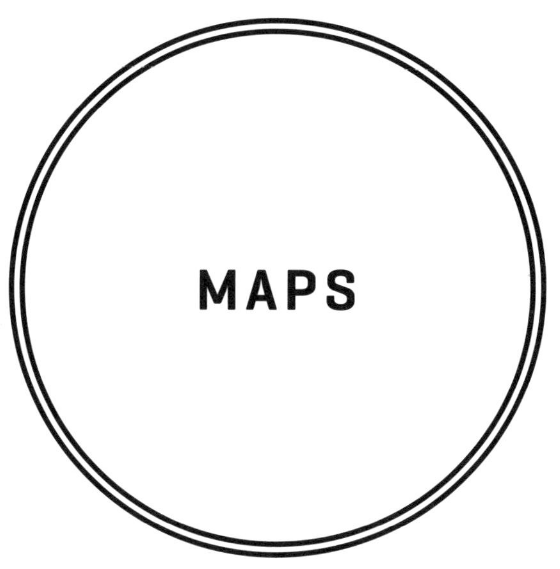

Pictorial journeys through unique Charleston culture, commerce and landscapes by local agency SDCO Partners. Not to scale.

PROGRESSIVE SUPPER

* JOHNS ISLAND

The Glass Onion

1219 Savannah Hwy

Rodney Scott's BBQ

1011 King St

* FOLLY BEACH

1870 Bowens Island Rd

Bowens Island Restaurant

* DOWNTOWN CHARLESTON
Xiao Bao Biscuit
224 Rutledge Ave
HANNIBAL'S
SOUL KITCHEN
16 Blake st
FIG
232 Meeting St
167 Raw
193 King st

PROGRESSIVE SUPPER

Imagine the ultimate Charleston tasting tour as one epic meal—or, better yet, a weekend's worth of dishes to try.

167 RAW

Oysters

A dozen of the day's freshest pairs perfectly with a seat at the bar and whatever's on draft from Charles Towne Fermentory. *193 King St*

BOWENS ISLAND

Frogmore stew

A simple mix of peel-and-eat shrimp, corn, sausage and potatoes. Sit on the porch and catch the sunset over the Intracoastal. *1870 Bowens Island Rd*

FIG

Tomato tarte tatin

The triumphant return of FIG's beloved tarte tatin, served simply with whipped chevre and cured olive, marks summer's arrival in Charleston. *232 Meeting St*

THE GLASS ONION

Shrimp and grits

The restaurant's take on this Lowcountry classic evolves with the seasons. But always, the shrimp are cut lengthwise so they curl into tasty ribbons. *1219 Savannah Hwy*

XIAO BAO BISCUIT

Okonomiyaki

"Cabbage pancake" may not sound compelling, but trust us. Topped with sunny-side up egg, kale, scallions and furikake. *224 Rutledge Ave*

HANNIBAL'S KITCHEN

Crab rice

Perfectly crispy blue crab over white rice—a Gullah Geechee favorite—is this low-key joint's signature dish for a reason. *16 Blake St*

RODNEY SCOTT'S WHOLE HOG BBQ

Whole hog pork plate

Beard Award-winning pitmaster Scott cooks his whole hogs low and slow—12 hours over the embers of burnt hardwoods—and it's worth it. *1011 King St*

FOOD WRITER *In Hanna Raskin's work, food is a vehicle for big societal questions. The longtime* Post and Courier *critic now writes* The Food Section, *a newsletter reporting on food across the South.* @hannaraskin

ARCHITECTURE

A tour of the city's most iconic dwellings, from colonial-period narrows to postcard-perfect townhouses.

FREEDMAN'S COTTAGE

Denmark Vesey House

This single-story cottage represents the kind of working-class architecture that Vesey, a freedom fighter and skilled carpenter, helped popularize. 56 *Bull St*

SINGLE HOUSE

Charles Graves House

One of Charleston's famously narrow dwellings, this Federal number occupies lots 226 and 227 on the colonial "Grand Modell of Charles Town." 123 *Tradd St*

DOUBLE HOUSE

Miles Brewton House

Owned by one family since 1796, this property is among the most well-preserved Georgia townhouses in America. 27 *King St*

TENEMENT

Cabbage Row

Formerly enslaved people once hawked produce from the tenement's windows. Today, the building holds private homes and fancy shops. 89-91 *Church St*

DEPENDENCY

Bennett-Simons House

Though hidden from view, outbuildings, such as these circa-1802 carriage and kitchen houses, were essential antebellum status symbols. 64 *Montagu St*

TOWNHOUSE

Rainbow Row

Originally built as live-work spaces for early merchants, these 13 oft-painted buildings make up the longest cluster of Georgian row houses in the country. *East Bay Street and Tradd Street*

PLANTATION

Drayton Hall

Only plantation on the Ashley River to survive both the Revolutionary and Civil wars. It owes its longevity to seven generations of heirs. 3380 *Ashley River Rd*

UNIQUE DESIGN *Only in Charleston will you find the single house, a form of two-story home characterized by its narrow profile [its name comes from the fact that it's only a single room wide] and side porch.*

Plantation House

Freedman's Cottage

Dependency

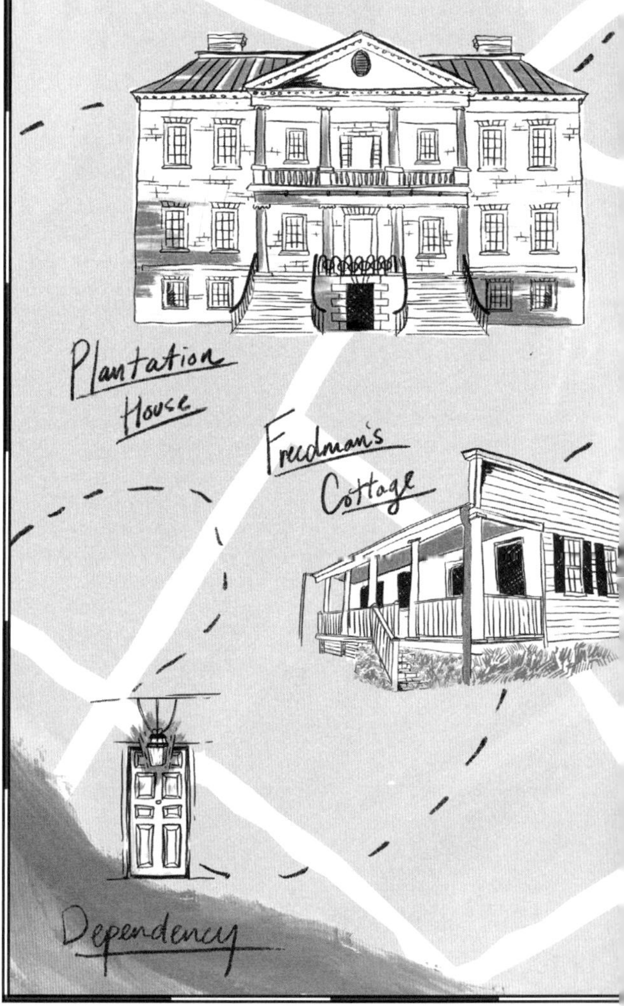

Townhouse
Tenement
Single House
Double House

Bertha's Kitchen

Mcleod Plantation

Joseph Fields Farm

Charleston Activist Network

CHARLESTON ACTIVIST NETWORK

Mother Emanual AME Church

Neema Fine Art Gallery

BLACK VISIONARIES

From working the land to education and activism, Black resilience is a defining element of the Lowcountry's history and culture.

NEEMA GALLERY
Centuries after Antwon Ford's ancestors wove baskets to winnow rice, the sweetgrass wunderkind's sculptural works breathe bold new life into the ancient practice. 3 *Broad St*

MCLEOD PLANTATION HISTORIC SITE
County park helmed by a team that forgoes romanticism in favor of boundary-pushing, nuanced storytelling about the stark realities of plantation life. 325 *Country Club Dr*

AVERY RESEARCH CENTER
Under the tutelage of Tamara T. Butler, the longtime polestar for Black stories and artifacts aims to activate its archives for social change. 125 *Bull St*

JOSEPH FIELDS FARM
As stewards of Johns Island's agrarian traditions and community, Joseph and Helen Fields stand for food accessibility and offer apprenticeships to the next generation of farmers. 3129 *River Rd, Johns Island*

MOTHER EMANUEL AME CHURCH
Plans for social justice and racial equality programs—rooted in talks with family members of 2015 massacre victims—reflect a mighty legacy of resistance and perseverance. 110 *Calhoun St*

BERTHA'S KITCHEN
Gullah Geechee soul in stewpots and steam tables. Founded in 1979 by the late Albertha Grant, whose three daughters carry on her legacy with each serving of oxtail, okra soup, lima beans and red rice. 2332 *Meeting Street Rd*

CHARLESTON ACTIVIST NETWORK
Founder Tamika Gadsden is a ringing voice for cultural change in Charleston. She also hosts the weekly [and self-described unapologetic] *Mic'd Up* podcast. *charlestonactivistnetwork.com*

UNTOLD STORIES *At the site of Gadsden's Wharf, where enslaved Africans first disembarked, the International African American Museum will shed light on lost family histories. iaamuseum.org*

ART INSTITUTIONS

Traditional and experimental, storied and fresh: Charleston's vibrant art scene runs the gamut.

GIBBES MUSEUM OF ART

The grand beaux arts building has been telling the story of art in Charleston since 1905. The collection features the works of local artists, including world-renowned Jill Hooper and rising star Fletcher Williams III. 135 *Meeting St*

HALSEY INSTITUTE OF CONTEMPORARY ART

Originally established as a gallery, the Halsey at the College of Charleston has evolved into a cultural touchstone: a multidisciplinary laboratory, where innovative art is both made and shared. 161 *Calhoun St*

REDUX CONTEMPORARY ART CENTER

Free rotating exhibitions alongside 40 affordable studio spaces for emerging artists. The center also hosts art classes [oil painting, figure drawing] as well as lectures by artists and curators. 1056 *King St*

CANNON STREET ARTS CENTER

This city-run cultural hub with a focus on community engagement opened in 2018 in a converted church. It includes a 110-seat theater [home of the ensemble Pure Theatre] and exhibition space. 134 *Cannon St*

ANN LONG FINE ART

Founder Ann Long Merck gathers works of contemporary realism—portraiture, landscape, still life—from points near and far. Specializing in artists inspired by the "slow art" approach to painting. A favorite among collectors. By appointment. *annlongfineart.com*

HELENA FOX FINE ART

A South of Broad gallery featuring the work of impressionists, realists and more. Come for the Lowcountry landscapes by artists including West Fraser and Julyan Davis, jewelry by goldsmith Sarah Amos and silversmith Kaminer Haislip, and more. 106-*A Church St*

PERFORMING ARTS *Held annually in late spring, the 17-day Spoleto Festival focuses on music and the performing arts. But it's a key connector in the wider world of the arts in Charleston. spoletousa.org*

ART INSTITUTIONS

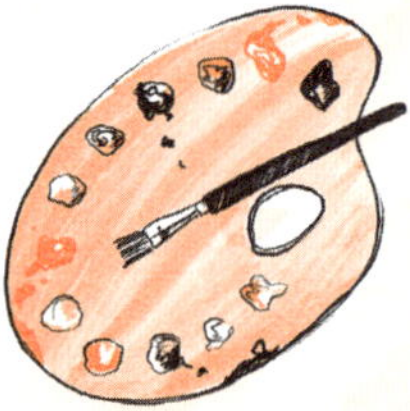

Cannon Street Arts Center

134 Cannon St

Gibbes Museum of Art

135 Meeting St

Helena Fox Fine Art

106-A Church St

Redux Contemporary Art Center
1056 King St
161 Calhoun St
Halsey Institute of Contemporary Art
* at the College of Charleston
Ann Long Fine Art

BEACHES

Seabrook Island

Kiawah Island

Edisto Island

Isle of Palms
Dewes Island
Sullivan's Island
Folly Beach

BEACHES

Along Charleston's barrier islands await boneyard beaches, world-class golf courses and alligators aplenty.

DEWEES ISLAND
Strict building restrictions, no cars along crushed limestone roads, and ferry-only access protect this tranquil sanctuary both 12 miles north of Charleston and a world away.

ISLE OF PALMS
A popular pick for families thanks to an abundance of activities and swells suited for beginners. Separated from the mainland by the Intracoastal Waterway.

SULLIVAN'S ISLAND
Refreshingly residential, the island is home to a palmetto log fort for American patriots, the last major lighthouse built in the United States, and a dense maritime forest that buffers erosion and storm surge.

FOLLY BEACH
Known for its funky-casual feel and for the Washout, best surf break in Charleston. Killer view of the 1876 Morris Island Lighthouse too. Find everything from surf wax to spam sliders along main drag Center Street.

KIAWAH ISLAND
The oak-lined approach of Bohicket Road sets the tone for Kiawah's natural charms. Golf rules here, with seven choices for a tee time, including the famed Ocean Course. Gator sightings are the norm.

EDISTO ISLAND
Serene and secluded. Where beachcombers can often spot sharks' teeth at low tide and Botany Bay's boneyard beach evokes a wild, otherworldly beauty.

SEABROOK ISLAND
Private beach with a full-service equestrian center [take your pick: trails or beach] and the first golf facility in South Carolina to join the Audubon Cooperative Sanctuary Program.

BEACH EATS *With its weatherworn salvaged-wood interior, Jacques Larson's Italian-inflected Obstinate Daughter is the perfect post-beach stop: local ingredient-fueled pastas, wood-fired pizzas and cocktails.*

SECRET GARDENS

Walk the historic South of Broad streets and peek into the enchanting arrays of jasmine, azalea, hedge and wrought-iron handiwork.

HEYWARD-WASHINGTON HOUSE, C. 1772
The Charleston Museum owns this property, where oyster-shell pathways, a riot of seasonal plantings, and scene-stealing camellias channel the 18th century. 87 *Church St*

CAPERS-MOTTE HOUSE, C. 1745
This layered double lot features a kitchen garden, a formal garden, and a stable garden brimming with giant roses; an old poolside privy functions as a potting shed. 69 *Church St*

THOMAS ROSE HOUSE, C. 1735
In the 1950s, landscape luminary Loutrel Briggs carved out garden rooms from a newly acquired adjoining lot and installed formal statues of summer and winter. 59 *Church St*

JAMES VERREE HOUSE, C. 1754
Emily Whaley chronicled her devotion to this secluded oasis in her bestselling memoir *Mrs. Whaley and Her Charleston Garden*. 58 *Church St*

GEORGE MATHEWS HOUSE, C. 1743
Climbing Iceberg roses, tulips, palms, ginger lilies, crape myrtles, azaleas and irises produce an Impressionist painting's worth of color. 37 *Church St*

WILLIAM GIBBES HOUSE, C. 1772
Briggs' first commission in Charleston, this property contains a rose garden, a central pool, and a sprawling lawn leading to the original summerhouse out back. 64 *South Battery*

PINEAPPLE GATES HOUSE, C. 1800
In recent years, a team of historians and experts unearthed this garden's original footprint—a series of three connected "rooms" meant to be viewed aerially from upper-level porches. 14 *Legare St*

GARDEN TOURS *Each fall, the Preservation Society of Charleston offers weekly garden tours in various neighborhoods. Visitors get to peer into private piazzas, porches and gardens.* preservationsociety.org

Pineapple Gates House

c.1800

14 Legare St

William Gibbes House

c.1772

64 South Battery

George Mathews Hous

c.1743

37 Church St

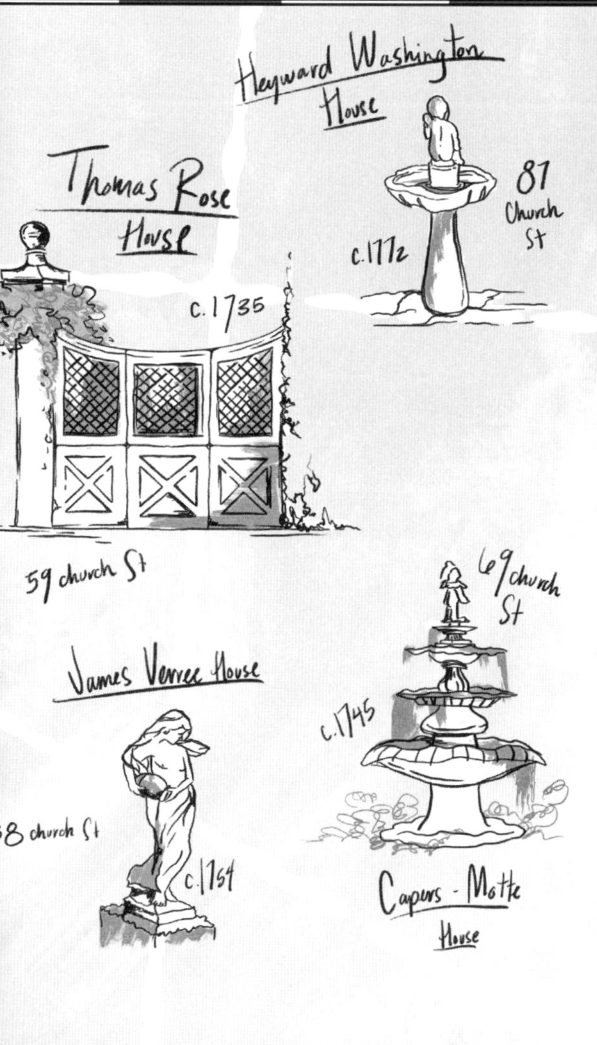
Heyward Washington House
87 Church St
c.1772
Thomas Rose House
c.1735
59 church St
69 church St
James Verree House
c.1745
58 church St
c.1754
Capers - Motte House

Thirteen conversations with locals of note about taxidermy, camellias, surfing, design, historic preservation, rice, silversmithing and tides

BECCA BARNET

TAXIDERMY ARTIST

THE TRICK is to double bag them so they don't get freezer burn.

TAXIS is to arrange and derma is skin. Literally, you're moving the skin.

BIRDS are heavily protected. If a cardinal dies, I can't touch it. The only birds I can have are chimney sweeps and starlings. I can have as many as I want.

I WAS A VEGETARIAN for six years.

WHEN I LIVED in New York, I worked with an insect pinner named Oscar. He was this big, burly dude with huge hands, and he pinned all the butterflies at the Museum of Natural History.

I DROVE down from New York with my two pet rats, Foxhunt and Fishhooks.

I KNOCKED on every door. The Aquarium, the Charleston Museum, the Children's Museum, the Halsey Institute.

NO ONE knew what to do with me.

BIRDS are the easiest. Get all the fat off, wash it with Dawn soap in water, and put it in a trash bag with Borax, corn grit and diatomaceous earth. Double-knot the bag. Then put it in the dryer for 15 minutes.

YOU'RE POLISHING the feathers and drying the skin and running the risk of ruining your dryer.

I GET my butterflies from a guy who collects them off the rainforest floor. I'll send him $100, and he'll send back whatever he can.

I HAVE A FRIEND who just gave me two piglets, a beaver and two baby lambs killed by a coyote. They're in my freezer. [*Opens freezer.*] What do you want to see? Coyote skins, a golden pheasant, a baby goat?

PRESERVATION is on the mind in Charleston.

YOU CAN'T PAINT a door here without getting it approved.

LINARD MCCLOUD

BAND DIRECTOR

I GREW UP right across the street from Burke High School.

I KNEW I WANTED to become a band director when I was in the ninth grade.

I DON'T KNOW that I was a prodigy, but I played in the band and I did enough to earn myself some scholarships.

I STARTED AT Burke High in the summer of 1978. The band had gone through a lot of directors at that time, but it was more or less in transition.

WE'VE GOT A practice class before school for the music, and then we practice performance after school.

CHARACTER IS the most important thing in a musician.

I DON'T LIKE to listen to music in the car, but if I do, it's going to be something by Beethoven or Mozart. Or Whitney Houston—I never listened to her music until she passed.

SUCCESS IS NOT determined by where you come from, but from how much respect you show for authority and how much respect you show for yourself.

WHETHER IT'S TO help them become movie stars, go to college, go in the military, do something positive with their lives, I try to pull out the best in my students.

THE MARCHING BAND is the darling of the school. They've given us the name "The Real Deal on Any Field."

DURING FOOTBALL season, we try to do something different every game.

MY FAVORITE MARCH is Heed's "In Storm and Sunshine."

THESE KIDS ARE proud of what they do.

THEY'RE A BUNCH of showmen, and they know that when it's time to show, it's a big thing.

KELLY KANE WOOD

SURFER

I'VE ALWAYS loved the water.

I'VE ALWAYS HAD the drive to be in the water instead of sitting on the beach doing nothing.

BUT I WAS horrible at surfing at the start. Terrible. Awful.

I BROKE MY nose getting slapped in the face by a longboard.

THE WHOLE REASON I started competing was so that I could spend Saturdays on the beach instead of working.

THE SURFING community is huge, and the girls are even tighter.

I DON'T HAVE too many problems with people in the water. I just paddle away from them if they're a bother.

PEOPLE HAVE BEEN surfing on Folly since the early 1960s. I have a chiropractor who surfs. My dentist surfs. My OB-GYN surfs.

MY FAVORITE time to go surfing is late morning. I don't wake up very easy.

A PERFECT WAVE is one that I get to catch from the beginning and ride to the end, and I don't bleed. Looking down the line of the wave and knowing where I'm going to go.

AND I LIKE TO surf very fast.

AT FIRST, I was scared to surf the Washout.

IT TOOK about four years before I would surf there.

I'VE SURFED through a lot of hurricanes.

SOME OF MY FAVORITE surf was during Earl. The waves were breaking past the last diamond at the pier—*at low tide*—which was huge.

I'M MORE AFRAID walking across Center Street than I am of sharks. Those drivers are crazy.

SIDNEY FRAZIER

HORTICULTURIST

I HAVE ALWAYS had a joy for working with plant material and working in the soil.

I WAS BORN and raised on a farm on James Island. Even then, I had my own little garden plot.

WHEN I FIRST came to Middleton Place in 1974 and got a job for the summer, it blew me away.

I NEVER KNEW a historic site like this was like right in my backyard.

AT MIDDLETON PLACE, you can look back in history and know that as magnificent as this garden is, it is because of enslaved Africans.

THEY WERE THE ones who landscaped this garden. They dug out the lakes and ponds and canal. They created the terraces and the garden rooms.

THE BONES OF the garden have not changed from 1741, when Henry Middleton married Mary Williams and they started landscaping.

MY RESPONSIBILITY IS to maintain the 65 acres of garden, lakes and ponds.

THERE ARE OVER 100,000 azaleas, over 10,000 camellias, and hundreds and hundreds of other plant materials that make up the garden.

THE CAMELLIA IS my favorite plant. One reason is that it flowers at a time of the year when nothing else is flowering.

THE PLANTS ARE like my patients. I monitor them, and I'm pretty good about catching things early on. I've been monitoring these plants for 47 years.

I AM JUST as excited to walk through this garden now as I was when I first started.

AND TO ACTUALLY see the plants change—a plant that was 16 feet in height 47 years ago is now 60 feet in height.

JUST TO KNOW that I was a part of that, it's incredible.

AMY PASTRE AND COURTNEY ROWSON

DESIGNERS

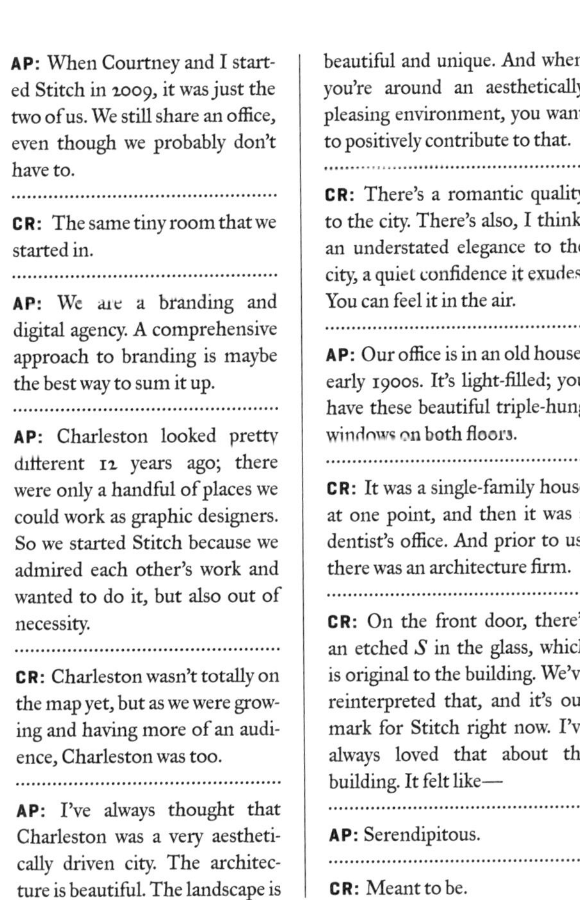

AP: When Courtney and I started Stitch in 2009, it was just the two of us. We still share an office, even though we probably don't have to.

CR: The same tiny room that we started in.

AP: We are a branding and digital agency. A comprehensive approach to branding is maybe the best way to sum it up.

AP: Charleston looked pretty different 12 years ago; there were only a handful of places we could work as graphic designers. So we started Stitch because we admired each other's work and wanted to do it, but also out of necessity.

CR: Charleston wasn't totally on the map yet, but as we were growing and having more of an audience, Charleston was too.

AP: I've always thought that Charleston was a very aesthetically driven city. The architecture is beautiful. The landscape is beautiful and unique. And when you're around an aesthetically pleasing environment, you want to positively contribute to that.

CR: There's a romantic quality to the city. There's also, I think, an understated elegance to the city, a quiet confidence it exudes. You can feel it in the air.

AP: Our office is in an old house, early 1900s. It's light-filled; you have these beautiful triple-hung windows on both floors.

CR: It was a single-family house at one point, and then it was a dentist's office. And prior to us, there was an architecture firm.

CR: On the front door, there's an etched *S* in the glass, which is original to the building. We've reinterpreted that, and it's our mark for Stitch right now. I've always loved that about the building. It felt like—

AP: Serendipitous.

CR: Meant to be.

BRIEN BEIDLER

BOOKBINDER

DAMAGE ON A book tells part of its story.

SAY THERE'S A book George Washington read, he got upset about something and threw that book against the wall, and the cover got damaged.

YOU WANT TO preserve as much of that damage as possible.

I AM THE chief bookbinder for the Charleston Library Society.

MY PERSONAL interest lies in medieval book structure.

YOU CAN LOOK at a book from the mid-1800s, and the leather will be cracked and the boards will be bent. And then you look at a book from the 1450s, and the leather's in perfect condition, the pages clean and white.

SOMETHING WAS LOST in the industrial revolution.

SINCE MY sophomore year in high school, I knew I wanted to pursue bookbinding.

I WORK FULL-TIME, 9:30 a.m. to 5:30 p.m. everyday. We listen to the Harry Potter series on audiobooks, and that helps.

IN THE 1950S, paperbacks were just sort of glued together. I call these industrial books. Industrial books killed the old-school bookbinders for sure.

THAT SAID, if there's a book I really want to read, I'll buy the paperback.

I TRY NOT to be at all critical of other people—unless they're really snobby.

I LOVE USING raw materials to make my own tools. Shaping the wood to make an awl. Cooking down bone to make bone folders.

A BONE FOLDER is smooth and oblong, almost like a tiny surfboard. You use it for manipulating paper and leather: folding, creasing, scoring.

IT'S ALWAYS in your hand, regardless of the task.

GERMAINE JENKINS

CHIEF FARM OFFICER

I CAME TO Charleston in 2000 to go to Johnson & Wales. I studied baking, pastry arts and food service management.

I GOT A work-study job with the YMCA, cooking for kids. Those kids were my first honest critics.

IT WAS A good training ground, and it led to me becoming the nutrition coordinator for the Lowcountry Food Bank in 2006.

THE FOOD BANK got a lot of calls from the Chicora Cherokee neighborhood in North Charleston. I would just put food in my car and take it to them.

WE WEREN'T supposed to do that. But I did it all the time. I had experienced what it's like not to be able to feed your kids.

WE'D BOUGHT A house over here. So we were living in a neighborhood where folks were calling about a need for food. Meanwhile, I'm driving 20 miles out of the neighborhood to get my groceries.

I KNEW THE only traditional way this neighborhood would get a grocery store was if it gentrified.

SO I SET about figuring out, how do we make high-quality produce available to people who may have EBT, like I did?

I STARTED Fresh Future Farm in 2014. Our mission is to grow the quality of life that our neighbors deserve.

WHAT'S UNIQUE ABOUT the farm, beyond the fact that there's a grocery store on site, is that we don't use chemicals and we don't irrigate.

ALL OF THE stuff we grow and sell is super nutrient-dense—and none of it is more than 200 feet from the store.

MY GENERATION GREW up thinking there's some kind of shame in farm work, when it's the ultimate privilege and opportunity.

EVERYBODY WILL always have to eat.

CALDER CLARK

WEDDING DESIGNER

I MOVED to Charleston in 2003. I'm totally a newcomer.

OF ALL THE BRIDES I work with, no one ever lives in Charleston.

I WORK WITH some couples who have never even been here.

THE CHARLESTON GIRLS use their moms. Maybe it's like a blueblood thing and I'm on the outside.

THE WEEK of a wedding, I'm there with my sleeves rolled up to install, and I'm there with all the iPhones and tuxedo jackets that get left behind.

IF THERE'S AN AWARD for hospitality or charm—from Condé Nast to tiny newspapers in Mississippi—Charleston is going to win it.

CHARLESTON IS GENTEEL, but not in a way that's off-putting. It's not like there are mason jars and sweet tea in your face every day.

THERE IS a really cool tension in the city's juxtapositions.

CHARLESTON IS never going to be all things to all people.

CHARLESTON IS so cool and hip and progressive on one side. And historic and slightly stuffy and stiff—in a good way—on the other.

YOU COULD BE at The Ordinary on upper King and there is a dyed-in-the-wool Charlestonian, street named after his family and everything, slurping oysters next to a tech guy with a pencil mustache and jeans. And both of these guys are Charleston.

CHARLESTON IS SO HOT, it's smoking. I can't keep up. There's always a new little lunch club, a new French spot, a taco joint opening. It's hysterical in a town this size.

IT'S VERY GREEN and very lush. Something is always in bloom.

JOE MCGILL

REENACTOR & PRESERVATIONIST

WHEN YOU put on a uniform and camp out at night on battlefields, it makes history more relevant.

I'VE BEEN a Civil War reenactor for over 20 years. I'm also a former employee of the National Trust for Historic Preservation.

I COMBINED my experiences into this thing I call the Slave Dwelling Project.

I'VE STAYED in 62 slave dwellings in 14 states.

IT USED TO BE hard to convince people to stay with me. Now I've got folks standing in line.

MY VERY FIRST stay was at Boone Hall Plantation.

I REMEMBER waking up around 3 a.m. to the sound of dogs barking and thinking that if it had been the time of slavery, that [sound] could possibly be slaves trying to escape.

NOT ALL of these places are located on plantations. In fact, many are in Northern states.

SOME FOLKS are surprised to hear that slavery existed in the North. It's no different than it was in the South; it just didn't take a war and the 13th Amendment to set things right.

WHEN IT COMES TO tourism, Charleston ends up on the "good" lists. But what I'm selling doesn't make good magazine material.

ONE OF MY traveling companions has slept in shackles. The first time he offered me the opportunity, I declined. I can't handle that.

I KNOW a lady who is spiritually connected who insists that the ancestors are guiding me to these buildings.

IF IT IS POSSIBLE to communicate with the ancestors, I wouldn't want to. They lived a life no one should've lived.

JOSEPH RILEY

LONGTIME MAYOR

BEING MAYOR is the best public service job in America.

TALKING is important because you have to communicate effectively, and be inspiring and convincing.

BUT IN THE final analysis, the job of mayor is a doing job. You either do it, or you don't. It either gets done, or it doesn't.

FORTY YEARS AGO, King Street was almost a ghost-town street.

FORTY YEARS LATER, Charleston is just wonderfully robust and, I believe, more beautiful than it's ever been at any time in its history.

WHATEVER you hear me say is something that, for good or for ill, I've prepared myself. I write all of my speeches.

I'M NOT a computer person. I go through about 80 to 100 black ink pens each year.

HUGO was one of the longest days of my career.

IN 1989, we didn't have the weather-tracking technology we have now, so we didn't know positively that Hurricane Hugo was coming directly here.

WHEN Hurricane Hugo hit and took the roof off of city hall, I told everyone, "Let's picture that we're in a war and the enemy is on the other side of the hill. If we let up for a minute, that enemy will come over the hill."

LISTEN TO PEOPLE. Always seek the truth. Work hard to understand the right course of action.

I'M ON a first-name basis with the city. It's personal.

I HAVE A 50-year test. Fifty years from now, will people be happy about what we're doing? Or is there a chance that people will say, "Why in the world did they back down?"

JASON STANHOPE

CHEF

I TOOK four months to drive across the country and stage at other restaurants. The whole time, I felt like I was biting my lip because I didn't think vegetables were being treated properly.

THE FOOD of Charleston has an identity.

PRESERVATION societies, coastal conservation leagues—they try to maintain the agriculture that's been important since day one in this city.

I COULDN'T find another place that compared to what FIG was doing. So I came crawling back.

LOCAL IS such an overused word.

WE ACTUALLY COACH our servers not to use the word. When you start throwing it around, it makes you wonder: Isn't it *supposed* to be that way?

WE'RE WORKING WITH farmers on stuff for next year or the year after, not just to grow more vegetables, but vegetables we can sustain on the menu.

I'VE BEEN to every farm, chicken supplier and produce person we have. It takes time to manage these relationships.

IT'S LIKE having 17 girlfriends.

TAKING CARE of the ocean is so necessary, but we're also trying to figure out how to take care of the fishermen.

THE OCEAN is such a beautiful and unforgiving beast. I lived on a sailboat for three months and was scared of the ocean for a long time afterwards. I just recently sucked it up and started going out with our crabbers and fishermen.

MARK MARHEFKA is one of the fishermen figuring out what chefs want, going out on four- to five-day fishing trips, instead of eight to nine, so restaurants can get fish more regularly.

WE'VE BEEN brought some fish that was so fresh, we couldn't serve it on the first day. It was still in rigor.

THE SO-CALLED trash fish are incredibly delicious.

OLD SOUTHERN delicacies like amberjack and porgy—if we treat them right and cook them properly, they'll keep us eating fish without depleting the ocean.

WHEN YOU BUY 400 pounds of fish, you're going to have 100 pounds of bones.

IT'S A HEALTHY trend to figure out how to use everything and minimize waste. I've seen the FIG menu morph over the years as a result.

RICE IS probably my favorite thing in the world, especially Carolina Gold. It is the most floral, nuttiest, starchiest rice I know.

IF YOU HAVE RICE at FIG, that rice is probably only a week old.

GLENN ROBERTS at Anson Mills is growing, preserving, harvesting rice on a large scale so restaurants can get it fresh. I put in an order; they mill it, separate it, pack it and send it to me.

RICE LED TO all these other things: Sea Island red peas, petite rouge, purple cape beans. The peas and beans were meant to make the rice better agriculturally, to put nutrients back in the soil.

A LOT OF US are putting rice in the middle of the plate. It's not just for filling up the bottom of a soup.

I THINK there's something pretty believable and genuine about eating food from your region. It's something you can't quantify in a recipe.

Jason Stanhope is the executive chef at FIG, which opened on Meeting Street in 2003. In 2015, he won the James Beard Award for Best Chef: Southeast. Stanhope was the fourth Charleston chef to win the prestigious honor, a list that includes Mike Lata, the owner and founding chef of FIG.

KAMINER HAISLIP

SILVERSMITH

BEFORE the Civil War, Charleston had one of the most prolific silversmithing communities in the country.

I FIGURED if silversmiths could be successful here 300 years ago, I could probably make a go of it today.

I'VE PROBABLY made a thousand pieces—tea pots, coffee pots, baby gifts, Christmas ornaments, salad servers, bowls, vases, jewelry.

IF you can dream it, I can make it.

THE SHAPE of my hammered rice spoon—which I call Flight of Fancy—is based on a bird's wing.

I MADE a cello-shaped broach for a client's sister's 60th birthday. The pin only ended up being about 2 inches long. To do the little strings on the cello, I used silver wire, drilled miniscule holes, pulled the wires through and then welded them onto the back. It was very nerve-racking.

I DESIGN FOR PEOPLE who saw their mothers and grandmothers entertain with silver, but who want to do it in a way that speaks more to their generation.

ANYTHING that's a little bit off-beat is oddly accepted in Charleston, even celebrated. When I lived in Charlotte, the joke would be, "Well, what bank do you work for?"

I WANT to bring silver down to earth and dispel the notion that silver is not a modern material, or that only the super wealthy can afford it.

I'M NOT a night owl.

I GET UP at 5:30 every morning and go to the gym. That gets me mentally ready for the day.

THREE-DIMENSIONAL objects are different from, say, a painting. You interact with them, use them, and that requires a different kind of thinking. Are they comfortable to hold? Do they function successfully?

DAVE BELANGER

CLAMMER

MY DAYS are dictated by tides and wind.

OUT WHERE I AM, on the edge of a huge wildlife refuge, you see the same birds, the same dolphins, even the same sea turtles.

YOU ACTUALLY get to know the individual wildlife.

THE SECRET to my success? Algae.

BROWN WATER is not so much fun for swimming at the beach, because you can't see your feet. But it's an excellent ecosystem for shellfish.

EIGHTY PERCENT of my customers are James Beard chefs.

THE PEOPLE I get along with the best are the pickiest and hardest to please.

CHEF MIKE LATA took my oysters and smoked them on hay. At Two Boroughs Larder, Josh Keeler had them on his menu from when he opened. He probably did them a thousand different ways.

WE DON'T sell oysters by the bushel; we sell them by the piece.

I CLEAN my oysters and clams thoroughly. Either I'm floating them on the surface for a few days after they come out of the mud, or I'm subjecting them to a pressure washer.

I HAVE a 22-foot Carolina skiff. It's like a pickup truck on the water.

BEFORE I MOVED to Charleston, I managed a 5,000-acre cattle ranch in southwestern Virginia.

IT STILL TUGS on my heartstrings.

I'M NOT FOND of seafood in particular.

THAT, IRONICALLY, has driven the quality of my business: If I like it, then it's probably pretty good.

INCLUDED

STORIES

Essays and selected writing from noted Charleston voices

FAMILY SUPPER

Written by **JOSEPHINE HUMPHREYS**

MY SHARPEST MEMORIES of a childhood in Charleston are mostly connected to food. I've always been a hungry sort of person, for food itself and also for what it means—family, place, stories, romance, history, the pure mystery of being. I can even be hungry for hunger.

When I was growing up, our midday meal was called "dinner." In the 1960s, that would change, as Charleston's unique traditions started to fray and dinner became the more American "lunch." Our dinner-time was two in the afternoon. We all ate in the dining room, my parents home from work for the dinner hour and we three daughters back from school. Our old table of dark mahogany, set with the worn "good china," had belonged to my grandmother. Early afternoon sunlight slung itself across the room. Outside, streets were empty, since everyone else was home for dinner too. We said grace, "Lord-make-us-thankful-for-what-we-are about-to-receive" [a puzzle, because how could you be thankful if you didn't know what was coming?] and then sat quiet, napkins in our laps. It was a curiously still and perfect moment, and somehow poignant, as if it might not come again. I felt a hard-to-describe longing, an ache vaguely like homesickness. Something seemed missing, something was in danger. But then we passed around the platters of food and the stillness broke. We ate, joked, teased, squabbled, swapped stories, and I was comforted.

At supper [later renamed "dinner"] we ate in the kitchen with mismatched plates and floral glasses that peanut butter had come in. Again we chattered our way through the meal. Town gossip, family rumors, news of the day, our parents' memories, tales from school—nothing seemed to be off limits. We were bound by food and stories, to each other and to our place and past. It seemed to me there was never a dish served that had not been served before, and never a good story that didn't get repeated sooner or later. Everything was literally familiar, that is, "of the family."

Mama [who would become "Mom" around the same time dinner and lunch were switched] was not the greatest cook in the world, to put it mildly. But I didn't know that then. Everything tasted good to me, even though her collards were boiled down to a soft mush and her rice was undercooked. Yet earlier in her life, she had been editor of a cookbook, the first version of the classic *Charleston Receipts*, and had called upon her friends and cousins to contribute recipes, including those for roast possum and squirrel. *Charleston Receipts* then expanded and became the bible of Charleston cooking, instructing Charleston homemakers in the proper preparation of traditional Charleston dishes like red rice, blue crabs, okra, civvy beans, sweet potatoes, benne wafers, Hoppin' John, and hominy [today called "grits"].

Canned goods figured in our diet, but so much of our food was fresh and local, I thought of myself as ingesting the Lowcountry itself. And a major portion of what we ate was free. We didn't have a lot of money, the family and all of Charleston having barely recovered from the Depression, even into the late 1950s. On top of that, my parents were serious penny-pinchers. Daddy [later "Dad"] grew scuppernong grapes and tomatoes, and hunted and fished to supply our protein—rabbits, wild ducks and, occasionally, marsh hens [clapper rails]; fish, shrimp, crabs and, once, alligator. I didn't have a steak until I was in college and a boy took me out to a steakhouse. I fell in love with him for that and eventually married him, but as a child, my only steak-like food was from deer my father killed.

The old standard method of hunting was called a deer drive. Three or four men with shotguns took up different stands in the woods, each leaning idle against the trunk of a pine tree until a deer came his way. On a proper drive, the deer were flushed by a pack of deer-hounds let loose on the other side of the woods. But Daddy and his friends didn't own any hounds. For dogs, they used us. Mama and her girls would walk through the woods whooping and shaking beer cans full of rocks, the deer supposedly fleeing ahead of us toward hunters and disaster. I was sickened the first time we were successful and I saw the result. But I helped with the skinning and gutting, and the cooking and eating.

I helped too with the shrimping, learned early how to untangle creek shrimp from the drop net, and later how to throw a cast net and pull a seine. We had cane poles with floating bobs for fishing, and we knew how get a whiting off the hook, tie a ripened chicken-back to a crab line and capture the crab with a scoop net, or call Daddy for help with catfish and stingrays. We could cook and pick shrimp and crabs before we were 10 years old. Boiling crabs was even more ghastly than gutting a deer, as the scrambling crabs had to be dumped live into boiling water. But those were the necessary processes. We knew first-hand the sources of our dinner.

If Charleston food linked me to the land—ocean, creeks, woods and farms—it linked me also to the town. Black vendors rolled carts through the streets selling vegetables and fish, and cooking aromas escaped from open kitchen windows, before air-conditioning came along. Home cooking was serious for everyone, and restaurants were few and far between. But on special occasions, our grandmother would treat us to dinner at Everett's, where the Black chef, William Deas, served up his specialty, she-crab soup. We loved that soup, my grandmother especially, because her bowl came with a glass of sherry to pour into the soup. Sometimes William Deas himself would step out from kitchen to say hello, all dressed in white. One day I looked up at him as he stood close to my chair, and I realized that I knew nothing about the real lives of Black people.

IF CHARLESTON FOOD LINKED ME TO THE LAND–OCEAN, CREEKS, WOODS AND FARMS–IT LINKED ME ALSO TO THE TOWN.

There was a whole half of my town that I was missing. The phrase was contradictory but exact—a whole half. We were utterly divided.

I didn't even know that Black families ate the same foods we ate, much less that the recipes in *Charleston Receipts* were often theirs to start with, and that some of the typical ingredients were African in origin. I'd believed my parents had told me everything, but they had not.

Planters used to refer to enslaved people as their "family," in a sense of the word that strains credulity; and yet it's a thought-provoking and downright inspiring word. A city should be a family of its citizens. Charleston's Blacks and whites shared food traditions—but never shared meals. It was not until I went off to college that I had any friends who weren't white.

Change is slow and nearly invisible until suddenly it's fast and, often, a big surprise. In 1970, when I moved back to Charleston after college, the placc was different. Blacks and whites were going to school together, working together, eating in restaurants together. There was more money to go around. Houses got spruced up. And then the first Spoleto Festival came to town, with all the bizarre magic of a crazy three-week circus, returning every year and changing the city forever. New restaurants appeared, catering to sophisticated performers and artists and festival-goers. We learned not to clap between movements of a symphony, and how to read *The New York Times* over a cup of espresso. America had discovered Charleston, and vice versa. There was no going back.

Today, decades later, our old town is more beautiful than ever. It almost shines. Some parts are gone, but its essence remains—a lasting grace, tested but continuing.

The old classic dishes survived. There is still no better red rice than home-cooked from *Charleston Receipts*; restaurants don't even attempt it. But grits ... grits can be found in just about every eatery in town, cooked in dozens of different ways. Cheesed, fried, spiced, made into bread—every chef seems to want a signature grits dish. And they're all good.

You can walk the restaurant areas now and find amazing food on almost every block. The energy of the restaurateurs is stunning. Enterprising young folks might start with a cart or a food truck, then progress to a renovated building uptown. Abandoned gas stations are a favorite target for these hopefuls, some of whom will move on to a fancier place downtown, some of whom will disappear. In the old days, we had a couple of Italian and Chinese restaurants, but now there's hardly an ethnicity unrepresented. A recent houseguest who had lived some years in France told me she'd rather eat for a week in Charleston than in Paris. Charleston cuisine is more adventurous, she said over dinner in a crowded new place on King Street. How could I argue with that, when we were eating butter-poached cobia with eggplant purée, chickpeas, and Castelvetrano olives; tomato salad with pistachios and a dollop of white chocolate cream; beef rib loin with garlic, black rice, and chimichurri; bread made of grits and rye; and watermelon salad with pine nuts, goat-milk feta, sprinkled with delicate blue basil flowers from the restaurant's rooftop herb garden?

It was extreme, it was trendy, but also delicious, fun, hopeful and secretly still distinctively Charlestonian. Fish, eggplant, tomatoes, rice, grits, watermelon, all old standbys. The watermelon particularly interested me, because I knew of a friend's effort to rediscover and revive the heirloom variety called the Bradford watermelon, once the South's sweetest melon but gone nearly extinct. David Shields, a food historian, is one of a new cadre of enthusiasts who have sparked a food restoration movement of sorts. They hunt down seeds and revive old methods of planting and cooking. Shields is full of ideas and dreams, one of which came to fruition this year. With the help of several Charleston chefs and experts and supporting groups, he planned the reproduction of a remarkable feast that had occurred 150 years ago.

SHARING FOOD CREATED A NEW UNITY, AND WE WOULD NEED IT YET AGAIN.

Nat Fuller was a slave who was also a successful chef. He ran his own widely renowned restaurant, with a clientele that included the wealthy planters of Charleston. By the time the Civil War ended, the planters were no longer wealthy and the future of the whole South was in limbo. Fuller put together a feast of reconciliation, inviting his former white customers as well as the city's Black leaders. Shields felt that the time was right for another reconciliation dinner, with the anniversary of the war's end coming up. It was a massive effort, a luxurious banquet free of charge like the original, with 80 guests, Black and white. I was lucky enough to be invited, and it turned out to be the most memorable celebration I've ever been part of.

What David Shields could not have anticipated was that just days before the banquet, a Black man was shot in the back and killed by a white policeman in North Charleston, and the city was reeling. So the Nat Fuller banquet turned out to have special significance, bringing people together at a time of trouble and sorrow. Sharing food created a new unity—and we would need it yet again, only three months later when an even more horrific tragedy occurred, the racially motivated massacre of nine beloved members of Emanuel AME Church by a white stranger.

Engulfed in grief and horror, Charleston drew on its reserves of strength, its grace and, in no small measure, the spirit of Nat Fuller, for a period of self-examination, honoring the lost ones and looking to the future. There can be no full consolation, but there can be a longing for it and a determination to seek it. There can be meals shared and friendships made, as well as major reforms. I believe we will be moving forward into a shared future we create together, in this new old city.

Hungers still consume me, but they also feed me, here in the place I love with the people I love. I no longer feel I'm missing a whole half. I think about those moments of panic I sometimes experienced as a child, wanting to hold everything together forever. And so far, things have held together. The boy who bought me a steak is now an old man with an old wife; he tends my dad's grapevines, grows every vegetable under the sun and brings home fish [but no deer]. I am thankful, always, for what I have received and what I am about to receive. And I am not a bad cook, as it turns out.

JOSEPHINE HUMPHREYS is a Charleston-born writer. Her novels include *Dreams of Sleep, Rich in Love* and *Nowhere Else on Earth.* In 1984, Humphreys won the Hemingway Foundation/PEN Award. Her work has also been honored with a Guggenheim Fellowship and the American Academy of Arts and Letters Award in Literature. She splits her time between Sullivan's and Johns islands.

EDISTO

Written by **KATIE CROUCH**

WHAT I REMEMBER MOST about growing up in Charleston was getting out of it. My childhood—such a beautiful, loaded word—trickled through the late '70s and early '80s. The city, at that time, was not a particularly bustling place. We had tourists, sure. Mostly nice, curious people from Ohio poking their noses in our garden gates. Still, in the summer the town literally became sleepy, in that the heat pulled us down to bed for long, sweaty afternoon naps. Most houses didn't have central air-conditioning before the 1989 hurricane. Instead of the widespread, comfortable indoor chill we now take for granted, Charlestonians made do. We crowded into the room with the window unit, and if there were too many people in there, we went outside on the porch, found a shady spot and waited for the sun to go down. My brother used to lie on the floor and watch the ceiling fan until he got dizzy. I liked to put my head in the freezer. *Stop that,* Mom would say. The ice will melt. Ice was important. We put it in everything. Water, milk, lemonade, gin. I'd say we put it in our coffee, but those weren't iced coffee days. In the summer, it was Coke in the morning, big 7-Eleven cups of it that left pools of condensation on the table and in the car.

I am 41 years old, and I am up early in Bolinas, California. I am remembering. I have just returned from a work trip to London, and I'm tired in a way I haven't been in a long time. It's that anxious sort of tired, when your body needs to sleep but it can't, because the heart knows something bad is going to happen. It was even worse in England, probably because of the massive distance from my five-year-old daughter, whom I left at home. I can't say what this bad thing will be, as everyone seems healthy. My daughter, my husband, my parents. Yet every morning for the last two weeks in my luxury hotel room, I shot out of bed in panic, looking around in confusion. The anxiety lasted all day, so I overworked and walked around the city. Everyone was on the wrong side of the sidewalk, and the cars drove the wrong way, and the signs on the ground warned: *Look Right!* I was frantic to leave. This is the thing I'm trying to work out in my mind this morning. I'm home and everyone is safe and sleeping, but the dread, it's still here.

The need to get out of Charleston in the summer, that was different. Heat does not cause anxiety; it brings on torpor. And so everyone had two houses: one in Charleston, and one at the beach or in the mountains, where you could get some air. I need to couch this by saying my childhood was spent in the singular, moneyed hamlet that was South of Broad, Charleston. I am remembering what a child remembers, with a child's view. I now realized that not everyone had two houses. Not Henrietta, the Gullah woman who raised me while Mom spent her days at the university. Not Mr. Singleton, the man who boarded up our windows before storms. Still, the other families who populated my small world, they made sure they had somewhere to go. A mountain house. A dock near the water. A slip for a boat. "Where's your other house?" we children would ask each other in the schoolyard. Lynnville. McClellanville. Pawley's. Drayton. Sometimes a kid with divorced parents would shrug and say: *We do time-shares.* But everyone, everyone went somewhere.

Each summer spot, of course, had its own flavor. Sullivan's Island, with its rambling old houses, was where the aristocratic families nested. Isle of Palms had some old houses too, but Wild Dunes brought in new-money families and renters. Folly Beach, well, that place was just a pure den of iniquity. As a teenager, my mother barely allowed me to go, even in the middle of the day. My brother, in his wild days, spent a year there he barely remembers. Even on Sullivan's, you could get a house cheap near the water, a plywood shack made mostly of screen. I wish I could say I was just being nostalgic, but these kinds of places just don't exist anymore near Charleston. Hurricane Hugo blew them down, and if not, they've been pulled down by a bigger, slower storm that doesn't have a good enough name. We just call it "Progress."

Our other house was farther afield—a whole hour by car—on Edisto Beach, a shabby stretch of houses and sand at the end of Edisto Island. This was seen by our South of Broad neighbors as an odd choice because of the distance and flavor, which indeed was more country

than genteel. My mother found an old beach shack that had once housed officers during the Second World War, when all of the beaches were used as lookouts for German submarines. My dad bought it for $14,000, which included the house, the lot next-door and two live oak trees.

Our "other house" was four rows back from the beach. It was a blue box with a sagging roof, linoleum floors and three tiny bedrooms. Frankly, it was a shithole, but it suited us. My mother filled the place with plastic furniture from Goodwill. There were no rugs, nothing you couldn't sit on in a wet bathing suit. You could eat anything in any room; dogs were allowed in and out at all times. There was one shower the size of a coat closet. The water was lukewarm and smelled dead. Box fans ran at all times, so that the sound was not of the ocean, but of an ever-throttling airplane.

Edisto Beach in 1979, it was not charming. It was not arrogantly shabby. It was a place where the white South Carolina lower-middle class came to drink while their children played and fought. The streets were mostly dirt. There was one paved road that ran down the center of the town. Trucks with monster wheels would cruise back and forth, their beds packed with drunken girls, their horns rigged to blare the beginning notes of "Dixie." There was a bar called Coot's Lounge where stabbings occurred with regularity. There were two restaurants, both of which served a limited menu of fried catfish, fried shrimp, fried hush puppies, beer, and liquor you could get in the back.

I am happy, if not proud, to report that in the decades since, I have witnessed people drinking on beaches all over the world. Men in Nantucket Red shorts sipping Dark and Stormys, yogis downing Singha in Thailand. In Bolinas, we drink red wine because it's foggy and we need something to warm our innards. Yet I've never seen alcohol prioritized in the way I remember it was on Edisto Beach in the 1970s. It was a prolonged, sustained activity that anchored the day. The cycle began at eight in the morning. Beachgoers would shuffle down, pitching umbrellas and dragging coolers. No one had figured out the suitcase-on-wheels concept yet. We often had friends with us to help carry the goods, but if not, this essential item was dragged by my father. I remember the sound of it, the scrape against the road, that ever-essential ice sloshing. Inside: Miller beer, some sort of punch not for kids, Fanta, Tab, mountains of bologna sandwiches in plastic baggies, one or two of which ended up floating belly up at the end of the day. As soon as we hit the beach, coffee ended and beer started. There were children and we were tiny, so to solve that problem, we wore life jackets so we wouldn't drown. If one of us was knocked down by a wave, we just relaxed and floated until someone noticed and fished us out.

And oh, the things we carried. I cannot remember the rest of my family's spoils, but my hump included, at different points of my adolescence: a pink inflatable horse, water wings, the aforementioned life jacket, an aluminum beach chair, a sodden towel, Betty and Veronica comic books, *Teen/Sassy/Seventeen* magazine, lip gloss, glitter lotion, lemons for my hair. Sunscreen was not required for anyone in the family other than myself, as I alone have pale, freckled skin. The SPF was eight and it stung and reeked of chemicals. The rest of the family wallowed in coconut oil or wore nothing at all. They turned a beautiful almond brown while I burned and blistered. I kept trying to tan, despite the obvious. A suntan in the 1980s, it was a thing of real value. Occasionally, my mother would bring graduate students down for the day. They would lather themselves up with Crisco, honest to God; it's amazing to have this memory, not just a fictional idea but a brain imprint of a nubile Latvian scientist applying shortening to her perfect skin.

The beach. You made your camp, you treated it like a home, you laid down and slept and drank and ate and came and went throughout the day, maybe to get more sand toys, or more chips, or more beer, or a different book. Weather-beaten, fat books. My father read *Shogun*. My brother read *Dune*. I read *Flowers in the Attic*. My mother read *Neuron*. Hours on the beach with a book, propping up on the elbows, then turning on your side, then stealing a chair when Dad went swimming.

I wore my first bikini at eight years old. This was normal. Everyone at Edisto started early in terms of the inappropriate baring of skin. I remember parades of teenage girls strutting up and down, glistening with oil and maybe Crisco, carrying beer in a Clemson coozy. My father's eyes, face—hell, his whole body—would follow their asses as my mother studiously ignored his ogling. Because ogling was okay. You were supposed to ogle. *Look at that,* my father would say to my six-year-old brother when a good bikini went by. So much value went into a well-worn bikini and a tan. Therefore: my first two-piece, green on my skinny, white, snap-bean body. *Seventeen* magazine

thrown open, legs spread-eagle in the sand. My mother glancing over, recognizing something I didn't understand. *You are not a teenager*, she barked, handing me a T-shirt.

So much happened. Everything changed. Yet days at Edisto Beach, they hovered, they crept by. You could lie on a bed and read half a book, listening to the beat of the box fan, and then get up and there were still hours of beach time left. If your parents were fighting in the morning, by afternoon they were either napping with the door locked, or the battle had mushroomed into threats of divorce. And once we were teenagers, the days were just torture. We wanted to be somewhere else, Sullivan's, Charleston, we didn't know where, but please, God, somewhere to whet our longings. I had one single-afternoon-long romance with a farmer named Walt. We kissed on a raft, and the next day he went for Mallory from Orangeburg, who was tan and filled out her bikini and had a beachfront house. I sat in my chair, watching them lord over us on her porch, and I wished and hated and wanted.

Am I romanticizing? Being sentimental? There were bad things. Awful things. My first corpses: a girl and a boy on a motorcycle, no helmets, headfirst into an oak on Highway 61, their deaths holding up Friday beach traffic. Don't look, my father instructed, so my brother and I fought for window space, and there they were, bodies, the pink froth of brains, a brown polished arm, long nails still glistening. There were parental battles, redacted. My brother and I betrayed each other weekly in ways I choose not to remember but still acutely feel. There was a black Lab we all loved because she would chase the ball for hours. Was her name Sally? *That Sally, she never gets tired!* We all liked to go to the beach before a storm because it was grey and green and lusty. And one afternoon right before the rain, our neighbors threw a ball into the ocean and Sally followed it, and the ball got caught in the current and Sally followed it, and the storm started and then Sally kept following the ball, and we all watched and screamed for Sally as she became a black speck in the churning sea and then went on.

My brother and I, we grew up. We went to college. The other house remained in the family, but without us it was just an accessory. In the city, air-conditioning happened. House prices went up. Families sold their Sullivan's and Folly houses and used the money to rest easy. My parents held on to Edisto for a while, but their weekend parties were now just kitsch. I'd come home to my parents' old friends drinking much

less than they used to, sitting on the beach watching the ghosts of their children, everyone relieved to go back home to a comfortable bed. I can't remember why or when my mother sold it. There was an episode where the family needed money, and once those sorts of things are over they are conveniently forgotten. And so the house went to another young family, who did a little bit to their other house, but really they don't seem very interested. I stop by when I'm out there and I peek in the windows. Maybe I've broken in once, as they haven't fixed that loose screen. There is new paint and a better floor and a big TV. It still smells bad. There is an outdoor shower, which is an excellent idea that I can't believe we never thought of ourselves.

My little girl is now stirring upstairs, and I am still tired, and I feel very far away from all of this. In a minute I will go up, I will get her dressed, I will make breakfast. But before that, this: I think when one grows up in the South, I mean, when one really breathes and bleeds it during the years she is becoming a person, that this has a lifelong effect. I don't know if it's good or bad, but it's something. And sometimes, if circumstances such as love and work cause her to land far away, she might encounter unexpected, acute bouts of mourning.

My childhood on Edisto Beach was not perfect, but it was thick. And when I return, all I see is the good. The family, all of us, has taken to renting a beachfront house like Mallory's every August. My husband, he tolerates our vacations there, but he points out what's obvious to someone who spent summers on Martha's Vineyard and Lake Michigan. That there are better places. Places without jellyfish, places with more diversity and culture and sailing and cooler air. The food is greasy, the houses look cheap, the sand is chunky, the people are drunk and loud. I don't care. My brother and I, we shuffle down at eight and pitch our umbrellas. We roll down the cooler [it has wheels]. We put our children in life jackets so we don't have to worry about them drowning. We sit there all day, reading and watching. And at night, finally, we sleep.

KATIE CROUCH is a novelist and essayist whose bestselling works include *Girls in Trucks* and *Abroad*. Her writing has appeared in *Slate*, *McSweeney's* and *Tin House*. Born and raised in Charleston, she now lives with her family in Bolinas, California.

SELECTED POEMS

As Charleston recovered from the difficulties of the Civil War and Reconstruction, the years between World War I and II represented a boom time for the arts, from architecture and historic preservation to visual art and poetry. It was during this time—known as the Charleston Renaissance—that a group of writers founded the still-vibrant Poetry Society of South Carolina. Below, a selection of poems by three of the society's founding members.

DUSK

Written by **DUBOSE HEYWARD**

They tell me she is beautiful, my city,
That she is colorful and quaint; alone
Among the cities. But I—I who have known
Her tenderness, her courage, and her pity;
Have felt her forces mold me, mind and bone,
Life after life, up from her first beginning—
How can I think of her in wood and stone!
To others she has given of her beauty:
Her gardens, and her dim old faded ways;
Her laughter, and her happy drifting hours;
Glad spendthrift April, squandering her flowers;
The sharp still wonder of her autumn days;

Her chimes, that shimmer from St. Michael's steeple
Across the deep maturity of June
Like sunlight slanting over open water
Under a high blue listless afternoon.
But when the dusk is deep upon the harbor,
She finds me where her rivers meet and speak,
And while the constellations gem the silence
High overhead, her cheek is on my cheek.
I know her in the thrill behind the dark
When sleep brims all her silent thoroughfares.

She is the glamour in the quiet park
That kindles simple things like grass and trees;
Wistful and wanton as her sea-born airs,
Bringer of dim rich age-old memories.
Out on the gloom-deep water, when the nights
Are choked with fog, and perilous, and blind,
She is the faith that tends the calling lights.
Hers is the stifled voice of harbor bells,
Muffled and broken by the mist and wind.
Hers are the eyes through which I look on life
And find it brave and splendid. And the stir
Of hidden music shaping all my songs,
And these my songs, my all, belong to her.

DUBOSE HEYWARD was an author best known for the 1925 novel *Porgy*, later adapted into a play and then into the opera *Porgy and Bess*. This poem appeared in the April 1922 issue of *Poetry* magazine.

SWAMP LILIES

Written by **JOSEPHINE PINCKNEY**

Today I feel new-born, for I have seen
A stretch of cloistered wood thick-spread with green,
Where wet wild lilies grew on every side,
Streaming away—an immobile white tide.
Not as the sun that bursts upon our eyes
At morning, making glory of the skies,
But like the slow, pervading evening light
They filled the eye—a world of silvery white
Withdrawn and exquisite, as from the sod
They breathed the still inviolateness of God.

JOSEPHINE PINCKNEY wrote poems, essays and novels. Her works include the novel *Three O'Clock Dinner* and the poetry collection *Sea-Drinking Cities*. This poem appeared in the July 1921 issue of *Poetry* magazine.

WHITE AZALEAS IN MAGNOLIA GARDENS

Written by **BEATRICE RAVENEL**

Your images in water! Sea-shell gray
And iridescence; like the endless spawn
Of pale sea-jellies on a moonless night—
A milky way that glamours out of sight—
Something of sea and something of the sky.
Drawn from the earth as blossoming dreams are drawn,
Most strange are you in this, that dreams alight and fly,
But you dream on all your translucent day.

Sweeps of divinest nothingness, abyss
Of beauty, you are the stirred, subconscious place
Of flowers, you are the rathe and virgin mood
Of young azaleas.
                                        Where heaped branches brood
Like bathers, water-girdled to the hips,
Like Undines, every blossom turns her face
Groping above the water, with her parted, winged, insatiable lips,
Each for her soul and its white mysteries.

BEATRICE RAVENEL'S poems and stories appeared in the *Sewanee Review*, *Harper's Magazine*, *The Saturday Evening Post* and elsewhere. She published two poetry collections: *The Arrow of Lightning* and *The Yemassee Lands*. This poem appeared in the April 1922 issue of *Poetry* magazine.

INDEX

INDEX